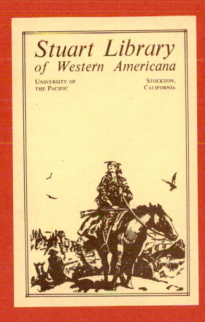

The Last Voyage of Thomas Cavendish
1591-1592

Thomas Cavendish. Anonymous. Courtesy of the Marquess of Bath,
Longleat House, Wiltshire.

The Last Voyage of Thomas Cavendish 1591-1592

The autograph manuscript of his own account of the voyage, written shortly before his death, from the collection of Paul Mellon

With an Introduction, Transcription, and Notes by

David Beers Quinn

Published for The Newberry Library by
The University of Chicago Press
Chicago and London

The Society for the History of Discoveries and The Newberry
Library wish to acknowledge the help of Mr. Paul Mellon
in the publication of this book.

The University of Chicago Press, Chicago 60637
The University of Chicago Press, Ltd., London

Library of Congress Cataloging in Publication Data

Cavendish, Thomas, 1560–1592.
    The last voyage of Thomas Cavendish, 1591–1592.

    (Studies in the history of discoveries)
    Includes index.
    1.   Cavendish, Thomas, 1560–1592.   2.   America—
Discovery and exploration—English.   I.   Quinn, David
Beers, ed.   II.   Newberry Library, Chicago.
III.   Title.   IV.   Series.
G246.C38A34   1975   910′.41 [B]   74–11619
ISBN 0–226–09819–2

Contents

Illustrations

Preface

Through the generosity and encouragement of Mr. Paul Mellon
it has proved possible for the Society for the History of Discoveries
and the University of Chicago Press to publish in facsimile the fine
autograph manuscript by Thomas Cavendish, written when he
believed himself to be dying on the Atlantic Ocean early in 1593.
The manuscript was brought to my attention in 1956 by Mr. Phillip
Robinson, who encouraged me to make a preliminary study of it.
The Robinson Trust subsequently sold the manuscript to Mr. Mellon,
in whose possession it is, though it will eventually adorn the Beinecke
Library at Yale University. Mr. Willis Van Devanter, formerly Mr.
Mellon's Curator and Librarian at Oak Spring, was the mainspring of
the plans to produce an edition of the manuscript. It has been possible
to add to the manuscript journal the original will, which has recently
become available: this has been done by courtesy of the Keeper of
the Public Records. Miss Gwenyth Dyke, Alison Quinn, Dr. Helen
Wallis, Mrs. Sarah Tyacke, together with a number of librarians,
archivists, and owners of manuscripts, have helped in the completion
of the work, as has Mrs. Sally Chidwick, formerly Secretary of the
School of History, University of Liverpool. Mr. Alan Hodgkiss drew
the track chart of the voyage. Rear-Admiral S. E. Morison USNR
(ret.) has sent some valuable comments. To all of them thanks are
gratefully given.

DAVID B. QUINN

Introduction

It is only very rarely that a manuscript of first-class importance for the Elizabethan period comes, newly, to light. Such, however, is the case with the holograph manuscript of Thomas Cavendish's personal testament and account of his last voyage, written at the end of 1592 for his friend and executor Tristram Gorges.[1] A copy came into the possession of Samuel Purchas, through the hands of Richard Hakluyt, and was published in his *Pilgrimes* in 1625, although with the suppression of certain passages.[2] The original manuscript appears to have been unknown to students of British overseas activity, until it now reappears after its long repose in the Phillipps Collection.

Of its authenticity and its outstanding interest there can be no doubt whatever. Cavendish was a leading member of the group of Elizabethans who pioneered the ocean sea routes of the world. His circumnavigation, if less novel than those of Sebastian del Cano and Sir Francis Drake, was an outstanding achievement. This manuscript, written in the utmost adversity on his last voyage, is not only one which contains information of substantial historical value but a remarkable human document as well. It brings to life, with all his gifts and failings, one of the more exceptional Elizabethan prodigies who, after a life of unusual achievement, wrote it shortly before he died—brokenhearted and in despair—in the wastes of the mid-Atlantic.

1. Formerly Phillipps MS 25851. It was apparently a late acquisition of Sir Thomas Phillipps and was not entered in his own catalog of his manuscripts, which does not go beyond 23837. It was given its present number in the unpublished handlist prepared by Edward Bond for probate in 1872 and was described simply as "Cavendish Voyage." It became the property of Messrs. W. H. Robinson and Co. Ltd. in 1946. Mr. Philip Robinson kindly provided what is known of its history while it was in Phillipps's hands, but the precise circumstances under which it passed from the Reverend Joseph Hunter (1783–1861) to Sir Thomas Phillipps (either directly or by way of an intermediary) are not known, while nothing has been learned about its earlier provenance.

2. Richard Hakluyt acquired a copy, presumably after he had published *The principal navigations, voiages, traffiques and discoveries of the English nation*, 3 vols. (1598–1600), which was seen by Samuel Purchas before he published the second edition of his *Pilgrimage* in 1614. Purchas noted (p. 863), "Apud Hakluyt I haue seen a Coppie of a discourse written by Master Candish himselfe to Sir Tristram Gorges whom he made sole executor of his last will." This he acquired after Hakluyt's death, printing it in his *Hakluytus Posthumus or Purchas his Pilgrimes*, 4 vols. (London, 1625), 4: 1193–1201, but stating (p. 1191) that "Some passionate speeches of Master Candish against some private persons not employed in this action I haue suppressed, some others I haue let passe."

1

The historical importance of the voyage is that it was designed to open up direct trade between England and the Philippines, China, and Japan. The story of how and why this ambitious venture failed is here told by its commander himself, in language which makes the manuscript of the greatest psychological and literary interest. On his deathbed Cavendish is the complete romantic—or supreme egotist—judging the world well lost once success has slipped his grasp, but also determined to shed the blame on his companions. The interest of the manuscript as a relic of a typical man of the Renaissance is both personal and dramatic. For the historian of European overseas expansion, for the naval historian interested in the hazards as well as the delights of navigation in the sixteenth century, and for the student of cultural history, the manuscript has peculiar attractions.

The Manuscript and Its Authenticity

The manuscript is on paper, with a parchment cover. There are thirty-nine leaves, each 19.4 cm by 14.1 cm, in five gatherings of eights, with one leaf (probably a blank at the end) missing. The first two leaves are written on both sides, the remainder on the recto only, making forty-one pages of writing in all. The leaves are foliated from 1 to 38 in a contemporary hand, perhaps that of the author of the manuscript himself, omitting one leaf after fol. 7, and there are figures indicating signatures (toward the left on the top margin) at the beginnings of the second and third gatherings.

The watermark is evidently Briquet No. 7140, found on French papers between 1581 and 1639.[3] (The central circle in the watermark cannot be seen in full so that it is not possible to be quite certain that it contains the *fleur de lis* of the Briquet illustration.) The chain lines are uniform (about 2 cm apart). The paper is in fair to good condition apart from a few leaves. Fol. 1r. and a few edges are dusty; fols. 1–2 are a little weak at the edges, and fols. 37 and 38 are somewhat damaged at the right-hand edge and bottom corner. On fol. 37 this affects the last six lines of text, and on fol. 38 one of the signatures.

The manuscript is neatly written, with some alterations of words and interlineations, in a secretary hand, with seven place names in italic, while twelve words at the end and two signatures are also in italic. The writing area is generally consistent. Though margins are not ruled, a line of 11 cm, with little variation, is maintained. The vertical size is somewhat more variable, ranging from about 16.7 cm to 18 cm. But there is little variation in the spaces between the lines. The number of lines to the page varies from twenty-eight to thirty-five, but most pages contain between thirty and thirty-three lines, while there is no increase in the irregularity of the spacing toward the end of the manuscript.

The parchment cover is made from a deed roughly trimmed to fit the paper and is attached by a line of stitching about 0.7 cm from the left-hand edge. The bottom edge of the present front cover is very rough and slightly imperfect; the back has a number of holes and both top and bottom edges are imperfect. On the front is an inscription in pen by the nineteenth-century antiquary, the Reverend Joseph Hunter (1783–1861):

> Note—this MS is
> printed in the 4th Volume
> of Purchas' Pilgrimes
> Jos: Hunter

3. C. M. Briquet, *Les Filigraines,* 4 vols. (Paris, 1907; new ed., Amsterdam: Paper Publications Society, 1968).

On what is now the back, upside down,[4] there are three lines of writing, now almost illegible. The first two may read "T[homas] Cavendyshe [his l]ast voyage," and the third (probably in another hand) "written by [him in] 159[2?]." The first hand is nearly contemporary and could be that of Tristram Gorges, to whom it was addressed. The obvious conclusion would seem to be that these lines originally formed the title on the front cover and that at some subsequent time, before the manuscript came into Hunter's possession, the cover was reversed, front to back and upside down, not improbably because of the fading of the writing and the poor condition of the parchment in what is now the back, and possibly also because the manuscript needed to be resewn.

The inside surfaces of the deed which forms the cover contain writing in a court hand of the late sixteenth century relating to a transfer of land in Cornwall.[5] It is most likely to have been added by Tristram Gorges shortly after he received it in 1593.

The manuscript is twice signed by Thomas Cavendish on fol. 38 (though one signature is now defective), and there are several references in the body of the text to his writing of it—especially to his inability to go on holding his pen in his hand—so that the assumption would naturally be that the text was written throughout by Thomas Cavendish as well as being signed by him. This assumption can be justified, but not without some discussion, since very little else survives in Cavendish's hand. An important exception is the holograph letter (signed) which he wrote from Plymouth to Sir Francis Walsingham on 8 October 1588.[6] It is the only letter of his known to be in existence and is neatly written throughout in an italic hand, being signed and addressed in the same hand. There is a signature of his, also in an italic hand, to a bond of 28 May 1586,[7] and also four signatures (all in an italic hand) on deeds in the East Suffolk Record Office.[8] Nothing in Cavendish's secretary hand has hitherto been known, but, by a process of elimination, it can be shown that the secretary hand of the manuscript can scarcely belong to anyone else. Firstly, the signatures to the manuscript are certainly the same as those of the other extant examples. The general character and the detailed writing of the signatures is such that there can be no doubt on this point. There are a few small points of difference in regard to style and spelling, though few, if any, Elizabethans were entirely consistent in their signatures. Chronologically the forms of signature we have are "Thomas Caundyshe," 6 June 1583; "Thomas Caundysh," 16 and 18 February 1586; "Thomas Caundyssh," 10 and 28 May 1586, and 8 October 1588; and in the manuscript (late 1592) "Th. Caundyshe" and "Thomas C[   ]" (fol. 38). The abbreviation of the Christian name in one of the examples is the only feature in the signatures on the manuscript which is not found elsewhere and it is not significant.

A second point to be made is that if there is no doubt about the signatures to the manuscript there can be no doubt either about the twelve words in an italic hand which precede them. They are entirely

---

4. The back cover has now been restored to its original place.
5. See pp. 145–47 below.
6. British Library, Harleian MS 286, fol. 161. See pl. 1.
7. British Library, Additional MS 12504, fols. 301–2v.
8. Ipswich and East Suffolk Record Office, nos. 50/22/1.22 (1), 312/252, 312/256, 312/261 (see pl. 2). These were located by Miss Gwenyth Dyke, who provided the references. Additional evidence is provided by The Hague map of the circumnavigation (pl. 9), the names on which are in the same italic hand as is used elsewhere by Cavendish.

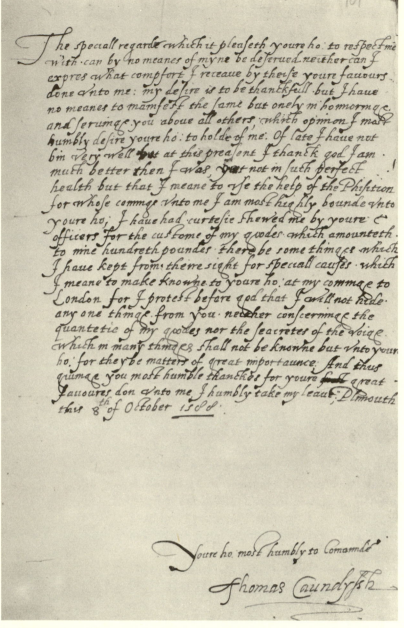

1. Thomas Cavendish to Sir Francis Walsingham, 8 October 1588. British Library, Harleian MS 286, fol. 161.

consistent with the signatures and with the text and address of the holograph letter of 8 October 1588, although they are written with a coarser pen than the latter and are very slightly simplified in form.

A third question then arises. Are the seven words which appear in the body of the text in an italic hand in the same hand as those at the end and as the hand of the 1588 letter? This cannot be stated with the same degree of finality, but there is little doubt that the answer is an affirmative one. The words are: "Caba bona Spe" (fol. 4); "Porte Sa Iulian" and "Porte desire" (fol. 7); "Porte desire" ([fol. 7 *bis*]); "Sainte Vyncent" (fol. 8); "Spiritus Sanctus" (fol. 13); and "Sainte Elena" (fol. 33); They correspond very closely indeed with the twelve words at the end of the manuscript and there is a reasonable degree of correspondence with the text of the 1588 letter.

This being so we can say with some confidence that the secretary hand, in which the body of the manuscript is written, is that of Cavendish himself and not that of an amanuensis, and that he is speaking literally when he concludes the text by saying, "beare with

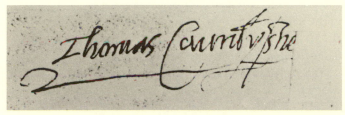

6 June 1583. East Suffolk Record Office, 312/261

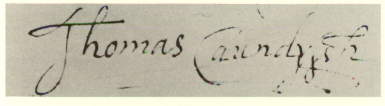

16 February 1586. East Suffolk Record Office, 50/22/1–22(1)

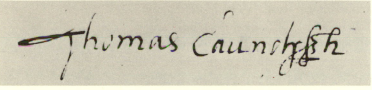

18 February 1586. East Suffolk Record Office, 312/252

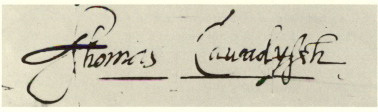

10 May 1586. East Suffolk Record Office, 312/256

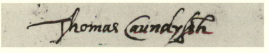

28 May 1586. British Library, Add. MS 12504, fol. 301

2. Cavendish signatures, 1583, 1586

this scribleinge for I protest I am scante able to holde A penne in my hand."

A final point must be mentioned, though here no certain conclusions can be drawn. There is clearly some discrepancy between the care, consistency, and neatness of the writing and the physical condition into which, according to the manuscript, Cavendish himself had fallen. A man who is dying at sea would not normally produce a document so coherent in form or, indeed, in logical structure. The critical word here is normally. Cavendish was a man of quite exceptional determination, and the character of the manuscript may well be a tribute to an iron will and an unyielding constitution. Or perhaps he was not physically as ill as he thought. Two things are certain. In the first place he had been suffering for some time from a degree of paranoia. In the second place he had determined to die—indeed he leads us to suppose that his intention had been, if he reached Ascension, to commit suicide. In these circumstances, the combination of a belief that he was about to die with the physical and mental strength to write the manuscript is credible. Neither of the explanations for the character of the manuscript indicated here can, in the nature of the case, be conclusive. But either would meet the case.

We can now take the matter further. As it will be shown, Thomas Cavendish wrote the manuscript not only or even mainly as a record of the voyage but as an apology for and an explanation of his failure to complete it successfully, and also, and most explicitly, as a guide to his executor, Tristram Gorges. Since the transfer of the early testamentary records of the Prerogative Court of Canterbury from Somerset House to the Public Record Office it has become possible to inspect not only the registered entry of the will and the proceedings leading to its probate, but the original will and the other associated documents.[9] His will is, in its handwriting and signature, identical with the manuscript which has just been described and endorses entirely the conclusions reached on such other evidence as has been assembled. It is signed by three members of the crew of the *Galleon Leicester* whom Cavendish trusted: Thomas Hammond, Stephen Seaver, and Robert Hues, the last being an able authority on cartography and navigation. In the proceedings before the court it was stated that "a wrightinge written with his owne hande"—the present manuscript—was "sealed vpp by master Thomas Caundishe in a Certaine Packett with his will which togeather with his will was deliuered close and sealed vpp to Tristram Gorge Esquier." It is probable that will and manuscript were secured by an outer waterproof wrapper which was sealed and which was not preserved. The manuscript and the will are reunited in this volume for the first time since 1593. Extracts from the narrative were written, by or for Gorges, on blanks in the paper containing the will, and these were accepted as a codicil to the will itself.

The manuscript was his vindication: it also attempted to salvage, for his heirs, his associates in the voyage, and his friends, the proceeds, if any, which survived the disaster which he felt was encompassing himself, if not necessarily all his companions, as he wrote. He wished in his last writings to emerge as the sacrifice of fate, but also as the avenger (as he thought himself to have been the victim) of the men he believed, however, mistakenly, to have failed him or betrayed him.

The Earlier Voyages of Thomas Cavendish

The laconic remark of Michael Oppenheim that "Thomas Cavendish of Suffolk was a circumnavigator of renown but he only copied Drake"[10] explains perhaps why the third commander of a successful expedition around the globe has not yet been accorded adequate biographical treatment or a proper place among the outstanding explorers of his time. Though Cavendish is known for the circumnavigation and for little else, he is, himself, a colorful and representative figure. He had something of the dash of Sir Richard Grenville though without his stability. Sir Humphrey Gilbert's overseas plans may have been more original and less practical than those of Cavendish, but the two men were similar in their violent tempers and uncompromising willingness to lose all if they could not

9. London, Public Record Office, Prerogative Court of Canterbury, Original Wills, PROB 10/Box 163, Thomas Caundish, 14 February 1595[–6] (facsimile and transcription on pp. 138–43 below). It seemed best to consider this manuscript after the other handwriting evidence as it is part of the same body of material as the subject of this volume, Cavendish's account of his final voyage.
10. *The Victoria County History of Suffolk,* ed. William Page, 2 vols. (London, 1907), 2:219.

achieve success. Like the Earl of Cumberland, Cavendish was a
rich young man who was determined to cut a figure in the new
dramatic and profitable field of privateering but who always retained
his amateur status: except possibly for drawing maps Cavendish
never learned to do anything superlatively well that had to be done
at sea; unlike Cumberland, however, he had a degree of tenacity that
enabled him, though he protested against his fate, to endure
hardship and difficulty. If he, in the main, had copied Drake in
1586–88, he proposed to do something new—to establish a trade
with the Philippines, China, and Japan—in 1591–92; and though
their ages and status were so very different, there are some
similarities in the tragic inevitability that seemed to dog both Drake
and Cavendish in their last voyages when nothing seemed to go
right and death crept in on both at the end. Cavendish was certainly
the most distinguished East Anglian of the overseas movement of the
sixteenth century and in the manuscript which he wrote when he
was near his death he has left us an intimate record which is
unparalleled by that of any other English navigator of the time.

Born in 1560 at Grimston Hall, Trimley, in Suffolk, Thomas was
the heir of William Cavendish, who died on 16 April 1572[11] when
his son was twelve years old. His mother, Mary, was a Wentworth.
After her husband's death she took Thomas to be brought up by
her brother, Lord Wentworth, at Nettleshead in the same county.
From there he went to Cambridge at the age of fifteen, entering
Corpus Christi College and leaving in 1577 without taking a degree.
It is not unlikely that from Cambridge he went to one of the Inns of
Chancery before enrolling at Gray's Inn and then attaching himself
to the royal Court in, or before, 1580. We have not, unfortunately,
any impressions of contemporaries on his rise in that large, expensive,
and highly competitive society where a young man might somehow
catch the notice of the Queen and come to the front, or else remain
one of the many decorative hangers-on. He had one advantage in
that he had a good income and was not, literally, hungry for favors
as were many of the other young gentlemen at Court.[12] Then too,
his sister Anne, two years younger than himself, managed to enter
the Queen's service and soon became a maid in waiting. Perhaps
Henry Seckford, one of the grooms of the Privy Chamber and a
relative, was the instrument for the advancement of both sister and
brother. Some patrons he must have had but we cannot say who
they were. Walsingham may have befriended him and, indeed, may
have helped to develop his interest in overseas ventures. Henry
Carey, Lord Hunsdon, is also most likely to have been helpful and
his son, Sir George Carey, certainly became a close friend. George
Clifford, Earl of Cumberland, two years his senior, overlapped with
him for a year at Cambridge and it seems probable that they were
friends and, in a limited degree, rivals. Somehow too Cavendish

11. The principal sources for Thomas Cavendish's early life are *Dictionary of
National Biography;* the Inquisition post-mortem taken after his father's death (PRO,
C142/162/151), where he is named as his heir and stated to be aged twelve years
or more; John Venn and J. A. Venn, *Alumni Cantabrigienis* 1, part i (Cambridge,
1922):311, where he is shown to have matriculated at Corpus Christi College,
Cambridge, in 1576; Gwenyth Dyke, "Thomas Cavendish and the Roanoke Voyage,
1585," *Suffolk Review* 1, no. 2 (1956):33–37; idem, "The Finances of a Sixteenth
Century Navigator, Thomas Cavendish of Trimley in Suffolk," *The Mariner's Mirror*
64 (1958):108–15, while I am also greatly indebted to the same author for the
opportunity of reading her unpublished "Life" of Cavendish.
12. After he reached his majority he took over his mother's lands in Lincolnshire
in return for the payment to her of a life annuity (PRO, Chancery Proceedings,
Elizabeth, C2/CC7/42, 20 March 1582 [–3]; his father's extensive lands in Suffolk
were by this time already in his hands.

must have got entry to the circle of the Herberts or the Sidneys, for he
first came to a degree of prominence when he was elected M.P. for
the borough of Shaftesbury in Dorset, inside the Earl of Pembroke's
orbit of influence, in 1584. That he retained that interest is shown
by his reappearance in the parliament of 1586 as member for Wilton,
the seat and center of Pembroke influence.

It was in the parliament of 1584 that the young Cavendish, now
in his twenty-fifth year, became closely associated with the group
of men who were most actively engaged in planning or executing
overseas ventures. One plan for such a venture which came up before
parliament in December 1584 was that of Walter Ralegh for
colonizing a recently reconnoitered part of North America. His
patent of 25 March 1584 was in general terms: he now wished to
have it confirmed by parliament so as to specify that
"Wyngandacoia," soon to be named Virginia, lay within its scope.
Like Sir Richard Grenville and several other M.P.'s, Cavendish was
drawn by Ralegh into the 1585 Virginia expedition. This was the
main result of the deliberations by the House of Commons on the bill;
it did not pass the Lords. Cavendish was designated High Marshal of
the expedition, and a series of notes on possible methods of military
organization and legal expedients, drawn up for Ralegh's voyage by a
military expert, were given to him. His task, an onerous one for so
young a man, was to act as the chief legal authority in the expedition
Sir Richard Grenville was to command and as such to be mainly
responsible for discipline on board ship and on land. He "Furnished
out" the *Elizabeth,* a bark of 50 tons, in which he sailed as captain.
To raise the money for the venture Cavendish mortgaged some of
his land to Humphrey Seckford and may have sold other portions of
it outright. Setting out from Plymouth on April 9, he was separated
from the other ships during a storm off Portugal and only rejoined
the *Tiger,* the flagship of the squadron, off the southwestern end
of Puerto Rico on May 23. Thereafter he sailed off to Hispaniola
with Grenville and eventually to the North American mainland
where the vessels anchored at Wococon in the Carolina Outer Banks
on June 26. He accompanied Grenville on an exploration of the
Carolina Sounds between July 11 and 16, and moved on to Port
Ferdinando, discovered as an opening in the Carolina Outer Banks
near the modern Oregon Inlet by the Portuguese pilot Simão
Fernandes in 1584, on July 27. There it was decided, first, to settle
on Roanoke Island inside the Sounds, and, secondly, to leave only
a small holding and exploring party on shore until the next year.
Whatever his intentions when he sailed, Cavendish was not intended
to be one of the 108 settlers. He did, however, remain behind until
September, after Grenville had gone, and he is mentioned by Ralph
Lane, who was to command the colony, as one who had fallen out
with Grenville during the outward voyage and who disapproved, so
Lane said, of Grenville's arbitrary actions on the voyage. It is not
at all unlikely that the young and fiery Thomas Cavendish took
unkindly to the manner and methods of his more experienced
commander. What we do not know is when the *Elizabeth* reached
home—not, probably, until the end of October or later.[13]

What did Cavendish gain from the voyage? Certainly much
valuable experience and an immense confidence in his own capacity
as a commander at sea, together with a determination to sail again

13. See D. B. Quinn, *The Roanoke Voyages 1584–1590,* 2 vols., Hakluyt Society,
2d ser., nos. 104–5 (Cambridge, 1955), 1:24, 130–39; 147, 174–75, 182, 190,
210–12; 214, 230, 266.

3. Thomas Cavendish. Engraving by Jodocus Hondius. From *Franciscus Dracus redivivus* (Amsterdam, 1596).

with no one as his superior. He gained too, if he had not already got it, the interest and support of Walsingham, and he was associated in the voyage with a number of men who were to be his friends and helpers later on: Captain John Clarke, who commanded another vessel for him in 1590; Captain Edward Stafford, who was to accompany him to Brazil in 1591–92 and to die there; and Edward Gorges, brother of the Tristram Gorges whom he was to make his executor and the recipient of his last confidences.

Within seven months after returning from the 1585 Virginia voyage Cavendish had built up a little squadron for himself and was preparing to emulate Drake and sail around the world. This reflects his exceptional energy and capacity, but it makes one wonder if this plan had been in his mind much earlier, before the Virginia voyage, or whether he received some other special incentive after his return. It may be suggested, though it cannot yet be proved, that the person who spurred him on was George Clifford, Earl of Cumberland. He and his wife knew Cavendish's uncle Richard, and Cumberland himself was restlessly looking round in 1585–86 for some overseas exploit to undertake. Ralegh, too, may have given encouragement, since he was to invest in Cumberland's voyage. This expedition was to enter the Strait of Magellan and to plunder the Spaniards in the Pacific and was in active preparation in the early spring of 1586.[14]

14. See S. E. Morison, *The European Discovery of America: The Southern Voyages*

For Cumberland to suggest that Cavendish might accompany or
follow him, with an eye to the ultimate union of their forces, would
not have been unlikely. Indeed, early in 1586, Cavendish was having
a new ship built, the *Desire,* of 120 or 140 tons. To her he added
two smaller vessels, the *Content* (60 tons) and the *Hugh Gallant.*
Cumberland's squadron was still in the Thames[15] when Cavendish
cleared on 10 June 1586, but his first stop was Harwich. It is clear
that he drew a good deal of his support and a number of his men
from his home county, and it is likely that he found it cheaper to
victual for a two-year voyage away from London or Plymouth.
Perhaps, when he set out again on June 27, he expected to meet
with Cumberland, who left Gravesend the day before, but Cavendish
got to Plymouth well ahead of him and sailed off on July 21,
Cumberland arriving soon after and leaving on August 17. Cavendish
left Sierra Leone, his first place of call, on August 29, while
Cumberland arrived there on October 21, so that Cavendish was
increasing his lead. Edward Fenton's expedition of 1582 had
prepared the way for this expedient, but that both Cavendish and
Cumberland made this call argues a possible agreement about routes.
Cavendish sighted Brazil on October 25, and on November 1
anchored in the channel between the Ilha de São Sebastião and the
mainland (lat. 23° 43′ S, long. 45° 24′ W), remaining there twenty-
three days, taking on water, fuel, and fresh food, and having a
small, 10-ton pinnace built on the spot. Setting out again, Cavendish
worked successfully past the Plate estuary and, putting in to the
Patagonian coast, found a harbor which he named "Porte Desier"[16]
(now Deseado, lat 47° 46′ S, long. 65° 54′ W, and first discovered by
Magellan), at which he found seals and, nearby, masses of penguins
on what is still called Isla de Pingüino. Storing a few tons of birds for
food, he pursued his advantage and on 6 January 1587, at the height
of summer, he passed Cape Virgins (which he renamed "Cape
Joy") and put into the Strait of Magellan. Cumberland was now far
behind, reaching the Brazilian coast (at 28° S) only on January 2
and, on February 15 (at 44° S), turning back for England, having
failed to make adequate provision for the voyage.

Making his way through "The First straight" (Outer Narrows)
Cavendish encountered a party of twenty-three Spaniards who were
all that was left of Sarmiento's colony of Ciudad Rey Felipe and
who were endeavoring, precariously, to make their way to the Plate.
One of them, Tomé Hernandez, was taken on board Cavendish's
ship.[17] They sailed on past "C. Deseado," "The seconde straight,"

(New York: Oxford University Press, 1974), pp. 709–19. Richard Hakluyt
printed an account by N. H. in *The principall navigations, voiages & discoveries of
the English nation* (1589), pp. 793–803, which he replaced by the fuller narrative
by Francis Pretty in *The principal navigations* (see n. 2 above), 3:803–25, and to
which he added Thomas Fuller's rutter (3:825–37). These are the basic
English sources.

15. The journal of the Cumberland voyage (British Library, Lansdowne MS 100,
fol. 23) says, "we loste the companie of *master* Candysh who departed from
plymothe 4 days before our comenge."

16. The names in quotation marks are from Cavendish's own chart of western South
America (The Hague map) with an enlarged inset of the Strait of Magellan (see pls.
9 and 10). The chart is discussed in Appendix III, below, as are the variations in
the complementary chart of eastern South America (the Florence map), which also has
an inset of the Strait (see pls. 7 and 8).

17. Tomé Hernandez (on whom see Richard Hawkins, *Observations,* ed. J .A.
Williamson [London: Argonaut Press, 1933], p. 105), in 1620 as an old man, gave
an account of his experiences at the hands of Cavendish. It was first printed in
Viajes al Estrecho de Magellanes por Pedro de Sarmiento de Gamboa (Madrid, 1768),
being added with separate pagination at the end, and was translated in *Narratives
of the Voyages of Pedro Sarmiento de Gamboa to the Straits of Magellan, 1579-1580,*
ed. C. R. Markham, Hakluyt Society, 1st series, no. 91 (London, 1895), pp. 269,

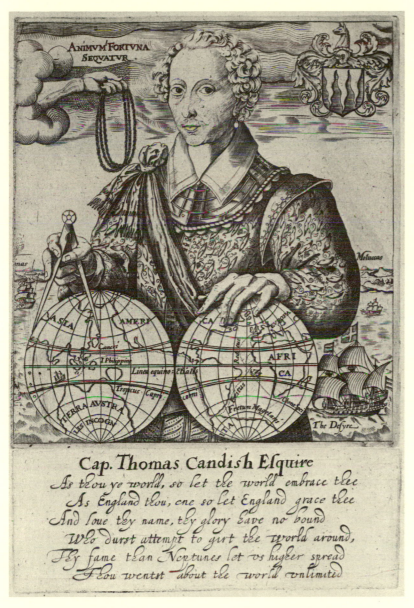

ANIMVM FORTVNA
SEQVATVR

Moluccas

The Defyre

Cap. Thomas Candish Efquire

As thou ye world, so let the world embrace thee
As England thou, ene so let England grace thee
And loue thy name, thy glory haue no bound
Who durst attempt to girt the world around,
Thy fame than Neptunes let vs higher spread
Thou wentst about the world vnlimited

4. Thomas Cavendish. Engraving by Robert Boissard. Bodleian Library, Oxford, Rawl. 170, fol. 121.

"Ylas de Penguines," "A great Gulet" (Useless Bay), until they came to the ill-fated Spanish settlement where over 350 people had miserably perished. Cavendish took half-a-dozen great guns as additions to his armament and christened the place anew as "Port Famin." At "Cape Frowarde" he estimated his latitude as 53° 40′ (for 53° 14′). Making good progress through Froward Reach and into Long Reach, they were then held up by contrary winds for nearly a month, in "most vile and filthie fowle weather," says Francis Pretty, but finally they sighted the outlet of the Straits, "a faire high Cape with a lowe poynt adjoyning unto it" (Cape Pilar and Cape Deseado), and so, on February 24, says N. H., "we passed out of the Straights into the Sea called by Magelan, Mare pacificum, the peaceable or the calme Sea."

Progress up the western coasts of southern and central America was slow—it took from 24 February 1587 to the following

November 4 to get to the California peninsula. The voyage was not
uneventful or unchallenged. First the *Hugh Gallant* was lost sight
of: she was not met with again for over 700 miles. Cavendish's men
went ashore at Isla Santa Maria (37° 48′ S) and at Isla Mocha (38°
12′ S), where they got fresh food. They touched at Concepción but
did not stay, and had their first tussle with the Spaniards at Quintero
Bay, near Valparaiso (33° S), where their prisoner Hernandez
escaped. Shortly after, watering on shore, their men were surprised,
twelve being killed and others taken. From there on they were to find
the Spaniards on the alert, with a system of warning boats and
messengers to keep ahead of the marauders. Cavendish thereupon
turned tough, seizing all the shipping he could lay hands on, whether
at sea or in the stocks, and destroying the vessels after taking anything he might need. At Arica they were especially successful,
capturing several substantial ships, but they failed to get the
Spaniards to barter any of them for their prisoners. One bark, taken
on St. George's Day, was christened the *George* and was brought with
them, while from a packet boat they took prisoners, whom they
tortured to give information on the letters they were carrying, and
also a Greek pilot, Jorge Carandino of Chios, who proved useful.
Between May 5 and 17 the vessels scattered as there was plenty of
spoil in the way of ships and food but little of greater value. In the
latter days of May and early in June the *Desire,* the *Content,* and the
George were all successfully careened and made ready for the crossing
of the Pacific at the Isla de Puna in the Gulf of Guayaquil (lat. 3°
S), though they had lost twelve men killed or taken in skirmishes
and accidents.[18] They decided to get rid of the *Hugh Gallant,* which
had evidently not stood up well to the voyage. North of the equator
they took another vessel from which they retained a certain Michael
Sancius (Miguel Sanchez, in Spanish) from Marseilles who had no
particular love for the Spaniards and who gave Cavendish, a little
later, the vital information he needed about the Manila galleon. In
the night Cavendish passed Acapulco (lat. 16° 48′ N), where he
might have had a rich spoil because it was the starting point and
terminus for the Manila galleon. He attacked, instead, the small port
of Aguatulco (or Guatulco), stripping it and destroying all of its
eight houses.[19] Armed with the information that a galleon was
expected, Cavendish then made his way north to await her, enjoying
good weather and finding useful harbors on the way. His men went
pearl-fishing with some success, while he careened his ship at
Mazatlán. He took up his station near Cape San Lucas on the southern
tip of Lower California on October 14 and on November 4 the
galleon was sighted at last. The *Santa Ana,* a 600-ton ship, repelled
the first attempt to board her. But two further attacks by the English
vessels forced her to surrender, since her heavy guns were in the
hold. For a fortnight this great ship occupied all the attention of the
Englishmen. Her company and passengers were landed at San Lucas
Bay and the ship stripped; 2,300 marcs of gold (102.3 lb. troy),
worth, in round figures, £70,000, were included in the ship's register,
together with an unspecified amount unregistered, as well as pearls,

18. For Spanish reports and reactions see Fernández de Navarrete, *Colección* 5: fols.
37–47; 18: fols. 257–59, 261–64; 18: fols. 128–91; *Colección de Documentos
Inéditos de Indias,* 2d ser., 21 vols. (Madrid, 1885–1928), 16 (1924): 47–48.
19. This episode, among others, is covered in Mexico City, Archivo de la Nación,
Inquisición tomo A, of which a copy is among the G. R. C. Conway Papers, no. 57,
Cambridge University Library, Additional MS 7282. In this series a number of
depositions taken at Acapulco on Cavendish's actions throw light *inter alia* on the
religious observances of Cavendish's men, and, especially, on those of his prisoners.

ARMIGER · THOMAS · CANDISH

Animum fortuna
sequatur

*Ignauos Fortuna fugit tu promtus in hos fes.
Pergis, et impauidus præda ditaris optima?* ℬ

5. Thomas Cavendish. Engraving from Henry Holland, *Herωlogia* (1620).
   Bodleian Library, Oxford, Antiq. C. X. 7 (4), opp. 88.

silks (raw and woven), satins, and damask, civet, and other
commodities.[20]

"This was," N. H. wrote, "one of the richest vessels that ever
sayled on the seas." But Cavendish was in a dilemma. He seems to
have lost or got rid of the *George* before this and he had not the crew
to man such a ship. His own two vessels must, perforce, carry mainly
food and water for the long transoceanic voyage. After a wrangle
with his men about shares, the valuables were disposed of, but what
was to be done with the rest? All the Spaniards were set on shore
and provided with the means to get to Mexican ports, but the great
ship and all but 50 tons of her cargo (about one-tenth of the total)
were set afire and burned to a hulk. She was the twentieth and largest

20. A few leading Spanish documents on the *Santa Ana* capture are printed in W. M.
Mathes, ed., *Documentos para la Historia de la Demarcación Comercial de California,
1583–1632,* 2 vols., Colección Chimalistac, nos. 22–23 (Madrid, 1965), 1:64–79.
A full account of the capture, though without specific archival references, is given
in William Lytle Schurz, *The Manila Galleon* (New York: E. P. Dutton, 1939), pp.
305–9. See also Césare Fernández Duro, *La Armada Invencible,* 2 vols. (Madrid,
1884–85), 1:152–56; Henry R. Wagner, *Spanish Voyages to the Northwest Coast of
America in the Sixteenth Century* (San Francisco: California Historical Society 1929),
pp. 150, 169, 187.

vessel to be disposed of, and the damage which Cavendish did to
Spanish commerce in the Pacific must not be underestimated. It was
a remarkable achievement for such a small force.

From his prize Cavendish took two Japanese (the Spaniards were
interesting themselves in Japan, where the Portuguese had had the
entry for some forty years), Christopher and Cosmus, as Cavendish
called them; three young boys born in the Philippines; and also a
Portuguese, Nicholas Rodrigo, who had been in Canton and elsewhere in China and Japan as well as the Philippines. It may have been
from him that Cavendish obtained the great map of China which
he was to bring to England.[21] Thomas de Ersola, as Cavendish knew
him (really Alonso de Valladolid), the pilot, another prisoner, who
knew the route to the Ladrones, proved very valuable also, since the
Desire made the passage in forty-five days, sighting Guam on 3
January 1588. The *Content* disappeared on the passage.

The climax of Cavendish's privateering plans came with the
capture of the *Santa Ana,* but the originality of his voyage lay in his
approaches to the Philippines and Java, for they laid the foundations
for his second voyage, which was directed toward these areas and to
the mainland of China and to Japan. The Spanish base at Manila
had set forth the fabulously rich galleon he had taken; therefore, even
if he dared not attack Spanish fortresses, everything he could find
about the Philippines was of potential value to him. Well guided by
his captives, he picked up Cabo de Espíritu Santo at the northeast tip
of the island of Samár on 14 January 1588, passed through the San
Bernardino Channel, and entered the Sulu Sea. He put in at Capul to
get refreshment after his long ocean traverse, and found the native
people cooperative both in bringing him supplies and in giving him
information about the Spaniards. Learning that his Spanish pilot,
Alonso de Valladolid, was attempting to send word of his activities
to Manila (he apparently succeeded in doing so), he had him hanged
out of hand. The *Desire* then worked her way westward to Masbate
and Sibuyan and, by the eastern end of Panay, into the Panay Gulf.
On the southern shore of Panay, at Arévalo (Caigoan), a recon-
naisance party almost took another Manila galleon. The *Santiago* was
nearly completed on the stocks there, and, if Manuel Lorenzo de
Lemos had not rallied the guard and chased the English party, the
galleon trade might have been disrupted for several years, but the
Santiago was able to take up in 1588 where the *Santa Ana* had left
off. A Spaniard, Lope de Arjoma, was taken prisoner, and from him
Cavendish learned something about Manila and of the island Negros,
to the south: he sent him off with saucy messages to Lorenzo de Lemos
and to the governor at Manila, Luis de Santiago de Vera, to the
effect that he would soon come back for more spoil.[22] This was, to
the haughty bishop of the Philippines, Fray Domingo de Salazar,[23]
the crowning insult. "The grief that afflicts me," he wrote to Philip
II, "is not because the barbarian infidel has robbed us of the ship
Santa Ana, and destroyed thereby the property of all the citizens; but
because an English youth of about twenty-two years, with a wretched

21. Hakluyt, *Principal Navigations* 3(1600):837–39, preserved certain details
from it.
22. Basic Spanish documents are in Emma Helen Blair and James Alexander
Robertson, eds. *The Philippine Islands, 1493–1898,* 55 vols. (Cleveland: A. H. Clark
Co., 1903–9), 7:52–111, and in Mathes, *Documentos* 1:80–95. See also Gaspar de
San Augustin, *Conquistas de las Islas Philipinas* (Madrid, 1698), pp. 435–36.
23. Blair and Robertson, *Philippine Islands* 7:64–68. See also Antonio de Morga,
Sucessos de la Islas Filipinas, trans. and ed. J. S. Cummins, Hakluyt Society, 2d ser.,
no. 140 (Cambridge, 1971), p. 68; *Colección de Documentos Inéditos de Indias,*
1st ser., 42 vols. (Madrid, 1864–84), 6(1868):466.

little vessel of about a hundred tons and forty or fifty companions, should dare to come to my own place of residence, defy us, and boast of the damage he had wrought. . . . he went from our midst laughing without anyone molesting or troubling him."

While warning messages went out from Manila to Spanish and Portuguese agents and outposts throughout the Moluccas, Amboyna, Java, and elsewhere, Cavendish sailed along the western shore of Mindanao and through the northern end of the Sulu Archipelago to coast Mindanao southeastward through the Basilan Strait to "Cape Cannal" (perhaps Tinaca Point at the southern tip of Mindanao) and then on a southerly course to the Moluccas, passing Gilolo at Cape Batochina (presumably a point on the western shore of Halmahera), but resisting the temptation to follow up Drake's more direct contacts with the Spice Islands. He continued his course, apparently through the Banggai Archipelago, and through the Banda and Flores Seas, until he reached the Strait of Lombok, through which he passed, leaving Bali to the east of him, to the south coast of Java. He was looking for a suitable harbor. He found one at Polambo, or Balamuao, at the eastern end of the island, where he made friendly and profitable contacts with the Raja Balamboam, trading for provisions and, perhaps, pepper.[24] There Cavendish also encountered two Portuguese factors, who expressed great interest in his tales of English support for Dom António and in his promise to come back to aid the Portuguese against the Spaniards. He asked them about the fortifications and resources of Achin and Malacca, and they also gave him much useful information on Java. He sent them off with church ornaments and other valuable presents from his loot and equipped them with letters to the bishop and captain at Malacca, saying he was coming to explore in that region; he also presented the Raja with three of his captured cannon. The Portuguese hurried off to Malacca to tell their tale, which was duly forwarded to Philip II by the governor-general at Goa, Manuel de Sousa Coutinho.[25] Cavendish finally set sail on 16 March 1588.

By these exploits Cavendish had considerably extended the picture of the Far East built up by Drake. Above all he had seized on the significance of the Spanish base in the Philippines as the key to trade with China, Japan, and other areas outside the Spice Islands proper, the main focus of Drake's activities. He had taken the opportunity to do propaganda with the Filipinos against Spain, and, indeed, conspirators in Luzon in 1588–89 cited his promise to return with aid against Spain. He had made useful trading contacts with Java and may have tried to stir up trouble there also for Spain. His contacts

24. The indications from Thomas Fuller and Francis Pretty that Cavendish sailed through the Strait of Lombok and along the southern coast of Java seem clear enough (Hakluyt, *Principal Navigations* 3:832–33, 822), but the location of Polambo and of the sultanate of "Raia Bolamboan" are not so easy to determine—it is given by the Portuguese as Balamuao (Blair and Robertson, *Philippine Islands* 7:52–53). P. A. Tiele, "Die Europeërs in Maleischen Archipel," *Bijdragen tot de Taal-, Land-, en Volkenkunde van Nederlandsch-Indië* 5 (The Hague, 1881):187–88, takes the Raja Balamboam to be the sultan of the state of Balambuang, located at the eastern end of the island and tributary to Surabaja. The name "Ballambaum" appears on the Peter Plancius world map of 1592 (F. C. Wieder, *Monumenta Cartographica*, 6 vols. [The Hague: M. Nijhoff, 1925–33], 2, pl. 34). The general location of Cavendish's landfall was thus in the vicinity of the peninsula of Blambangan at the southeastern end of the island, modern Banjuwangi and its harbor lying on the Bali Strait to the north and Gradjagan and its harbor on the south coast near the peninsula. The latter is a likely place for Cavendish's anchorage. It is possible that before leaving Java Cavendish sailed along the south coast and put in at another harbor there, toward the southwestern end of the island. B. Leonando y Argensola, *Conquista de Islas Malucas* (Madrid, 1609).

25. Blair and Robertson, *Philippine Islands* 7:52–53.

with the Portuguese were of the slightest but he found that another possible way to attack Philip II was through his unwilling Portuguese subjects in the East. Moreover, the ease with which Cavendish sailed through the complex of islands and channels showed that, with reliable pilots, which his proved to be, access to the Far Eastern islands was relatively simple, even though he appears to have been extremely fortunate in his winds and weather.

On March 16, again refreshed, the *Desire* set out on her long run to the Cape of Good Hope, and made the coast of Africa on May 14, some way east of the cape. Working around into the Atlantic the men made their way to St. Helena, calling there only twenty days after the Portuguese East Indies fleet sailed for home. On June 20 the *Desire,* which had proved an excellent sailer, set out on the last lap and, near home, heard from a Flemish hulk, the news of the Spanish Armada's defeat. A storm met them at the mouth of the Channel and tore their worn canvas to shreds, but on September 9 they worked their way into Plymouth, "like wearied men," returning, as Camden said, "with a rich Booty and great Glory, as being the second after Magellan who sailed round about the world."[26]

Thomas Cavendish put into Plymouth in September 1588 to find the country still ringing with the defeat of the Armada and, indeed, his own exploit was treated by the Queen as a happy appendix to that event. His earliest letter, written on September 9 to Lord Hunsdon, reflects his own exhilaration.[27] But he was busily occupied for another month with the assessment of the returns of the voyage, the payment of shares to the crew, the totting up of the customs duty (5 percent in cash), and the lord admiral's tenth (in kind), so that it was not until October 8 that he was able to write to Sir Francis Walsingham.[28] Cavendish says in this letter that he had been courteously treated by Walsingham's officials in regard to customs— special men would have been sent down—and that he had been charged £900 duty. This meant that the goods, apart from bullion and jewels which would be dealt with separately, were valued at £18,000 (which, with the gold, made a total of nearly £90,000). This is unlikely to represent the full market value of the silks, raw and woven, and the spices, but it was a rough approximation. Some things, Cavendish said, he had reserved from the officials, but he assured Walsingham that he would hide nothing from him, neither the quantity of goods "nor the secrets of the voiage." Some of the latter would be told only to Walsingham "for they be matters of great importance." These were most probably mainly about China as he had told Hunsdon he had brought "such intelligence" of that country "as hath not bene heard of in these partes." Rumor soon swelled the amount he was thought to have brought back. It was worth three million crowns; it included two ships filled with spoils; he was credited with seven prizes brought to port. It is not unlikely that among other things he was credited with other men's prizes. Soon estimates shrank to 500,000 crowns, a mere £125,000, and perhaps

26. William Camden, *Annals of Queen Elizabeth* (London, 1688), p. 397.

27. It was published in a pamphlet, with the date "M.D. LXXXVIII" but without place of publication or name of printer, entitled *Advertisment certain contenant les pertes advenues en l'Armee d'Espagne, vers le Noest, de la coste d'Irlande, en leur voyage intenté depuis les Isles du Nord, par delà l'Escosse envers Espagne. Et du nombre des hommes & navires perdus. Avec deux lettres, l'une d'un Flamen, Catholique zelé, demeurant à Londres, à un Seigneur Espagnol & l'autre de Monsieur Candiche, qui a passé le destroit de Magellan, pour aller aux Indes, & est retourné par le Cap de Bonne Espérance.* Copy in John Carter Brown Library, Providence, Rhode Island. It was again printed by Hakluyt, *Principall navigations* (1589), p. 808.

28. British Library, Harleian MS 286, fol. 161.

we might guess this was near the true figure. It was certainly a princely one.[29]

When the *Desire* was brought around from Plymouth to the Thames at the beginning of November she made a fine show: her men were decked out in silken damask and gold chains; her sails were of blue damask, and her standard of blue and cloth of gold; some regretted that her rigging too was not silken. Such Chinese luxury had not hitherto been seen in England. The vessel was sailed past the royal palace at Greenwich and the Queen was saluted with a salvo as the *Desire* came to anchor. She is reported to have said: "The king of Spain barks a good deal but he does not bite. We care nothing for Spaniards; their ships loaded with gold and silver from the Indies come hither after all." On the fifth day Cavendish gave a banquet for the Queen at which she made similar remarks. The great cabin was hung for the occasion with cloth of gold, and the flags, we are told, were marvelously rich. Rumors about the great spoil of gold began to grow again, but the Queen kept such things dark and, no doubt, took a great share of what her new young hero, still only twenty-eight years old, had brought two-thirds of the way round the globe.[30]

Not everything was as bright as Cavendish might have hoped. He might reasonably have expected knighthood at the Queen's hands (indeed he is often, mistakenly, referred to as Sir Thomas Cavendish), but she did not choose to honor him in this way. A more positive blow came when his £2,000 bond, under which he had undertaken not to interfere with friendly ships and to give a full account of his prizes, was estreated.[31] We do not know whether this was because of complaints about attacks he had made on merchant vessels on the way out—some of the five Basque Newfoundlanders he fought with may have been French ships—or whether he was found to have concealed some valuable prize goods from the royal officials. He may well also—since he got through what remained with such speed— have been obliged to hand over to the Queen an exceptionally high proportion of his booty.

Coming so soon after the defeat of the Spanish Armada in July, Cavendish's return in September was another blow against Spain —a second penetration by the English of her closed Pacific realm—and could be exploited for propaganda purposes. The letter which Cavendish wrote on September 9, announcing his return from his

29. The papers in *Calendar of State Papers, Spanish, 1587–1603* (London, 1899), pp. 437, 454, 473–74, 483, 486–89, 491–93, supply much of the surviving detail, though as the work of spies they are not likely to be wholly reliable in detail. See also *Calendar of State Papers, Foreign, July–December 1588* (London, 1936), p. 230; *The Fugger Newsletters, 1568–1605,* ed. Victor von Klarwill, 1st ser. (London 1924), pp. 126–27; Purchas, *Pilgrimes* 4 (1625): 1191.

30. Only the titles of popular ballads which celebrated the event have been preserved: "a ballad of maister Caundishe his voiage, who by trauel compassed the globe of the World, Arryving in England with habundance of treasure"; "A newe ballad of the famous and honorable commyng of Master Candishes shippe Called the 'Desyer' before the Queenes maiestie at her Court at Grenwich the 12 of november 1588"; "Roberts his welcome of good will to Captayne Candishe," in Edward Arber, ed., *A Transcript of the Registers of the Company of Stationers of London, 1554–1640,* 5 vols. (London and Birmingham, 1875–94), 2 (1875): 505, 506, 509. Robert Parke hurriedly dedicated to Cavendish his translation of Juan González de Mendoza, *The historie of the great and mightie kingdome of China* (1588), saying that he understood "that your worshippe in your late voyage hath first of our nation in this age discouered the famous rich Ilandes of the *Luzones,* or *Philippinas,* lying neere vnto the coast of China . . . and that also yourselfe haue sailed along the coast of China, not farre from the Continent, and haue taken some knowledge of the present state of the same."

31. The bond (British Library, Additional MS 12504, fol. 302v) is endorsed "Master Caundishes bond. and Stephen Hare to my lord Admirall in 2000. lib. forfaited." Stephen Hare, master of the *Content* on the circumnavigation, had been the joint signatory of the bond signed on 28 May 1586.

successful voyage, was used in this way.[32] The third circumnavigation, with its further proof of the vitality of English maritime activity, was thus given, if only in brief outline, a European currency.

Cavendish's career cannot, so far, be followed fully during the years 1588–91. Yet, if the years 1586–88 may be classed as ones of "getting," those that followed were clearly years of "spending." John Hooker says of him, dryly, "and allthoughe his greate welthe was thought to have sufficed for hym for his whole lyff, yet he sawe the ende therof within verie shorte tyme."[33] He had, of course, his lands to recover with some of the money and he seems to have invested vigorously in shipping. We do not know how much he had to do it with after his creditors and crew, not to mention the customers, the lord admiral and the Queen (interested especially in the bullion), had taken their toll. His energy did not abate, however, and as early as January 1589 a report from London told the Spaniards that he had nearly got the *Desire* in order again—probably an expensive business after such a long voyage—and had bought a smaller vessel and a pinnace; later messages said that the pinnace had foundered in the Thames with the loss of almost all her men and that Cavendish was having another built. The story the Spaniards collected was that he was about to set out for China and was working in collaboration with Cumberland, who was to keep company with him at least until they were through the Strait into the Pacific.

In May the center of interest shifted to Plymouth and there the two expeditions were said to be ready to set out, though it was Cumberland's alone which sailed on June 18. The Spaniards did not learn of this until after July 8 as, on that date, they were still writing of Cumberland and Cavendish being ready to leave, each with ten ships, the one to China, the other to the Moluccas.[34] Cumberland, whatever his original intention, went only as far as the Azores. What basis in fact the earlier rumors about him and about Cavendish had cannot be ascertained, though there is a certain plausibility about them. While Cavendish cannot have hoped to return in 1589 to the Philippines as he had promised, he might well have expected to set sail again in that year. He was unfortunate, however, since most of his country's maritime effort was being directed to the attack on Portugal, which achieved only very limited success. It is not unlikely also that the cancellation or postponement of Cavendish's plans was caused, in part, by unexpected delays in making the *Desire* seaworthy. On 22 December 1589 she was described as still being at anchor in the Thames.[35] What Cavendish did was to acquire a large privateer which he named the *Roebuck*. She was a vessel of 240 tons, carrying 20 guns and 100 men. Ralegh also had a ship called *Roebuck* and there was a London ship with the same name so that ships of this name are easily confused. The complaint put in by the Dutch about the *Roebuck* in 1589, however, relates to Cavendish's ship. It was said that she had

32. See note 27 above.

33. Exeter City Record Office, Book no. 51 (*sub anno* 1588). Gwenyth Dyke, "Finances of a Sixteenth Century Navigator," contains valuable details of what is known of his dealings in these years.

34. *Calendar of State Papers, Spanish, 1587–1603* (London, 1899), pp. 504, 511, 525, 531, 540, 548. Richard Hawkins, *Observations,* see n. 17, p. 11, confirms the loss of the pinnace in the Thames: otherwise it is difficult to separate fact from rumor in these reports.

35. PRO, High Court of Admiralty, H.C.A.1/42, 22 December, deposition of Richard Harrison referring to "the Deserte [clearly the *Desire*] belonging to Master Candishe." One of Cavendish's ships was robbed at Blackwall in the summer of 1590 (H.C.A.14/148, 17 August 1590).

taken a Dutch prize worth £1,462 and had brought her and her goods to Barbary for disposal.[36] We are left without further information on this venture, which, as described by the Dutch, sounds more like piracy than privateering.

We are on rather firmer ground about the activities of Cavendish's ships in the following year, 1590. By then he had acquired the *Galleon Dudley,* another large privateer, of 350 tons, carrying 120 men, and had put her under the command first of Captain John Clarke, whom he had accompanied on the Virginia voyage in 1585 and who was an old hand at the privateering game, and later of Stephen Seaver, who was to accompany him in 1591. The *Roebuck* had as her captain this year Abraham Cocke, an experienced privateer commander. Letters of reprisal were taken out in February for the *Roebuck,* and it is probable that while she was sailing under them she despoiled, illegally, two Irish vessels, the *George Cumberford* and the *Ross,* while a Portuguese prize with 550 tuns of wine and possibly other cargo was brought by her into Southampton on 10 July 1590. The *Galleon Dudley* had been one of the members of Grenville's Virginia squadron diverted by the Armada crisis in 1588. She was probably in company with the *Roebuck* when she took a Dutch or Flemish ship, and she, too, brought a prize—a Spanish vessel laden with hides—into Southampton in July. She was out again later in the year with her new captain, Stephen Seaver, and this time she took a valuable Portuguese brazilman (the cargo was worth at least £1,340), as well as seizing goods from another Flemish ship.[37] These ventures are not likely to have lost Cavendish money, but it cannot be proved that they brought him a substantial profit, since captains and crews had a way of dissipating proceeds before the owners who had not gone to sea with them could lay hands on the spoils. This in turn, however, implies that Cavendish himself did not go to sea in 1590, although, for lack of evidence, it cannot be stated categorically.

Undoubtedly, before the end of 1590 Cavendish was deep in the preparations for a new venture. He was determined that the bulk of the shipping should be his own. He disposed of the *Galleon Dudley* because she was not, in some way, satisfactory for his purposes, and bought a large veteran, the 400-ton *Galleon Leicester,* which he intended to command himself. He also acquired the *Black Pinnace,* the vessel which had earlier brought Sir Philip Sidney's body back to England. With the *Roebuck,* which Captain John Cocke was to command, and the *Desire,* once again ready, it was hoped, for an ocean voyage, he had four vessels with which to embark on his last and fatal enterprise. To them he added the *Daintie,* a small bark owned by John Davis (who was to command the *Desire* in the first part of the voyage) and Adrian Gilbert. Randolph Cotton was to go as her captain. On 24 June 1591 a royal commission gave him license to depart on his voyage, in the usual rather cryptic terms, "to enter and take in hand a voyage by Sea purposed by him tendinge to the service of us and our Realme and to the encrease of his owne knowl-

36. British Library, Lansdowne MS 145, fol. 83v.

37. See PRO, H.C.A.14/27, no. 12 (misplaced between nos. 72 and 73), 17 February 1590; *Acts of the Privy Council, 1590* (London, 1899), pp. 398, 465; H.C.A.14/27, nos. 86–88, 148; H.C.A.13/101 (under 16, 20, and 22 October, 28 November 1590); British Library, Harleian MS 598, fols. 7v, 10; British Library, Lansdowne MS 142, fols. 115, 354; Kenneth R. Andrews, *English Privateering Voyages to the West Indies, 1588–1595,* Hakluyt Society, 2d ser., no. 111 (Cambridge, 1959), pp. 143, 163–64.

edge, whereby he shalbe the better able hereafter to doe service to us and our Realme."[38]

Cavendish had gone, with his uncle Richard Cavendish, on 18 May 1590 to consult the famous Dr. John Dee,[39] most probably on the prospects of reaching the Pacific end of the supposed Northwest Passage. He had also received, in honor of what he had done and what he aspired to do, the freedoms of the boroughs of Southampton and Portsmouth.[40] He was now at liberty to depart.[41]

The Last Voyage

Cavendish had sailed around the world once. There is little doubt that he aspired to be the first man to do so twice. But this alone would scarcely have led him to embark on his last voyage. What did so was his expectation of repeating his previous success in plundering the Spaniards in the Pacific and also of doing something new, opening up direct trading contacts with China and, possibly, Japan, most probably by taking over the Spanish base at Manila. One of his treasured prizes found on the *Santa Ana* was the large map of China (from which Hakluyt preserved the nomenclature though the map itself appears to have perished). Moreover, he had with him in England the two Japanese, who now spoke English well and with whose aid, and that of the pilot Rodrigo, he might hope to overcome the language barrier and start an English galleon trade with China that might emulate the fabulously rich Manila galleon itself. Fenton had aimed at something of the sort in 1582, but had not reached the Pacific, and Cavendish had had it in mind in 1586, yet it now seemed a much more feasible project. There were, indeed, other expeditions in hand to reach the Far East by way of the Cape of Good Hope. Other adventurers, Lancaster, Raymond, and Foxcroft, got away by that route before Cavendish was ready to leave for the Strait of Magellan. Yet Cavendish had a third string to his bow. John Davis was persuaded to sail with him. According to Davis he consented to go because of his personal affection for Cavendish and against the advice of others of his friends. In fact, he did so with a different objective in mind. His remarkable voyages up the strait which still bears his name in search of the Northwest Passage to Asia in 1585–87 had taken him to latitude 73°N, and he returned convinced that the passage existed. Now he hoped to search for its Pacific end. The *Daintie,* jointly owned by Davis and Adrian Gilbert and equipped by their friends at the cost of £1,100, was to be detached, once the peninsula of California had been reached, along with Cavendish's *Black Pinnace,* to make the search for the Pacific terminus of the passage which Drake had failed to press home in 1579.[42] Davis's preeminent skill as a navigator and chart-maker was at Cavendish's disposal for the dangerous passage through the Strait. Plunder, trade

38. PRO Patent Roll (Watson's Roll), C.66/1606; copy in State Papers, Domestic, Elizabeth I, S.P.12/237, fols. 53v–54v.

39. John Dee, *The Private Diary,* ed. J. O. Halliwell, Camden Society, 1st, ser., no. 19 (London, 1842), pp. 33–34.

40. Historical Manuscripts Commission, *Corporations of Southampton and King's Lynn,* 11th Report, Appendix III, [series 18], (London, 1887), p. 21 (9 July 1590); *Portsmouth Records,* ed. Robert East, 2d ed. (Portsmouth, 1891), p. 137 (9 September 1590).

41. Sidelights on the preparations are in *Middlesex Quarter Sessions Rolls,* ed. John C. Jeaffreson, 4 vols. (London, 1886–92), 1:293 (misdated 1592 for 1591); George C. Williamson, *George, Earl of Cumberland, 1558-1605* (Cambridge, 1920), p. 310.

42. Dedicatory epistle by John Davis to Lord Howard of Effingham, in John Davis, *The seamans secrets* (London, 1595), sig. ¶ 2v.

and discovery, in that order but not necessarily with that emphasis, were thus the objectives of the 1591 expedition.

The expedition was long in preparation but we can pass over what is known of the minor hitches which impeded its sailing, remarking only that the victualing appears to have been badly done and the men perhaps exceptionally unruly. A feature of the expedition was the high proportion of soldiers, many of them gentlemen, to seamen. This was a familiar enough expedient for expeditions to the West Indies or the Main, but was probably unwise for such a protracted venture as Cavendish now envisaged, for in the long run it was the seamen who counted in getting the vessels home again. It might appear that the squadron was somewhat overmanned, even though a number of men had deserted at Plymouth.

On 26 August 1591 the *Galleon Leicester,* the *Roebuck,* the *Desire,* the *Daintie,* and the *Black Pinnace,* with some 350 men, left Plymouth,[43] being seen off by, among others, Richard Hawkins and Tristram Gorges. Their route took them down the Iberian shore and there, early in September, they met with a fleet of Flemish merchant-men returning from Lisbon. These seemed fair game; several were chased and one was captured. She turned out to have an English safe-conduct, was induced to part with some salt for payment, and provided the useful information that the Portuguese Brazil fleet had already left Lisbon and was not likely to impede Cavendish's vessels. Twenty days out, the Canaries were sighted but there were no prizes to be picked up on the island shores. This time there was no thought of touching at the West African coast. Cavendish set out to cross the ocean to Brazil but he misjudged the trade winds and was soon caught in the doldrums near the equatorial line and becalmed for twenty-seven days during which scurvy and fever did much damage among his crews. In these trying conditions an accusation by the two Japanese that a Portuguese pilot they had with them had tried to seduce them to run away in Brazil was taken so seriously by Cavendish that the Portuguese was tried and hanged. Eventually the southeast trades came to their rescue and twenty days' sailing brought them into Brazilian waters. On November 29 they entered a bay known as Salvador, midway between Cabo de São Tomé and Cabo Frio (lat. 23° S, long. 42° W). While they were awaiting a wind to bring them southward, a small vessel bound for the Plate was captured, from whose men they obtained some useful information.

Cavendish planned to sack the port of Santos and to use it as a base for equipping himself for the dangerous journey into the Pacific. He worked down the coast past Rio de Janeiro to Ilha Grande (known

43. On the early phases of the voyage John Jane's account (Hakluyt, *Principal navigations* 3 [1600]:842–52) is valuable, though in the later stages he deals with Davis's experiences which were not shared by Cavendish; Anthony Knivet (Purchas, *Pilgrimes* 4 [1625]:1201–42) is very helpful down to the time he was left ashore in Brazil. His account has been well edited (as *Vária Fortuna e Estranhos Fados de Anthony Knivet* [São Paulo: Editora Brasilense Limitada], 1947), by Guiomar de Carvalho Franco and Francis de Assis Carvalho Franco. Cavendish's own account, hitherto available only in the somewhat shortened form (Purchas, *Pilgrimes* 4 [1625]: 1192–1201), is the sole authority for the later phases of the voyage, though we lack evidence on the last stage of the voyage of the *Roebuck* and the *Galleon Leicester.* We have also an intercepted letter from John Vincent (alias John Yates), S.J., to Sir Francis Englefield, ca. June 1593 (PRO, S.P.12/245,33) giving some details from the Brazilian side. Detailed references are not given for every point, but quotations from the Cavendish manuscript are keyed to its foliation. On the physical setting Robert C. Murphy, *Oceanic Birds of South America,* 2 vols. (New York: American Museum of Natural History, 1936); Admiralty, Hydrographic Department, *South America Pilot,* parts 1 (9th ed.) and 2 (13 ed.) (London, 1942–45); Felix Reisenberg, *Cape Horn* (London: R. Hale, 1941); Richard Hough, *The Blind Horn's Hate* (London: Hutchinson, 1971); and Morison, *European Discovery of America: The Southern Voyages* have proved helpful.

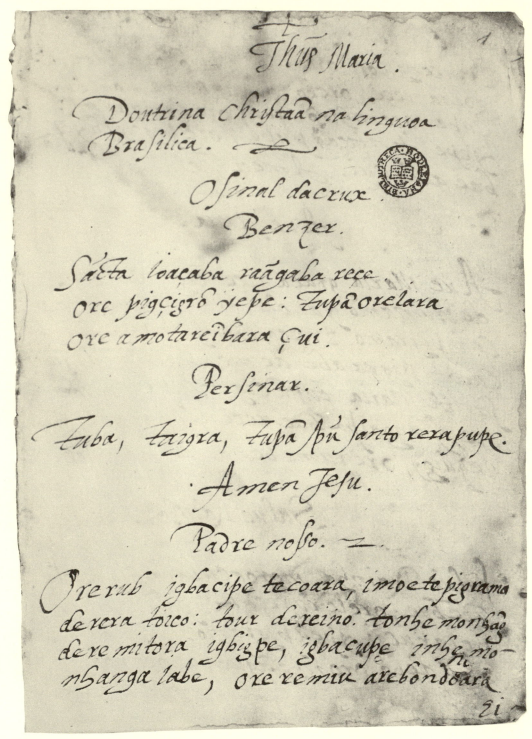

6. Title page of "Doutrina Christãa na lingua Brasilica," taken by Thomas
Lodge at Santos, 1591. Bodleian Library, Oxford, MS Bodley 617, fol. 1r.

to the English as Placentia), where he sent marauding parties ashore.
The men concentrated mainly on seizing fresh food, for which they
were ravenous. On December 11 the ships pushed on to Ilha de São
Sebastião and, while Cavendish lay in the roads there (Canal de
São Sebastião), the *Daintie,* the *Desire,* and the *Black Pinnace* were
detached to reconnoiter Santos. The *Daintie* entered the port in the
guise of a trader, as other English ships had done in the past,
and found no difficulty in getting a lading of sugar and other goods.
With the information she brought him Captain John Cocke was able
to attack the port with the other two vessels on December 16,
surprising the Portuguese at Mass and holding almost the whole of
the settler population as hostages. According to John Jane of the

Desire this coup was not adequately exploited since the local Indians were allowed to move freely in and out of the town and consequently were able to remove, under the eyes of the English, most of the food stored there. Cavendish, with the remainder of the squadron, arrived on December 22 and remained until January 24, a delay which some of the men regarded as prejudicing their chances of getting an easy passage through the Strait. All their foraging during this period does not seem to have produced a great deal of food, and the vessels were still inadequately victualed when they departed, leaving Santos and São Vicente largely ruined and a number of vessels destroyed in the Baia de Todos os Santos.

The stay at Santos had some literary associations. Cavendish took up residence for a time at the Jesuit College there with a number of gentlemen. One of them was the writer Thomas Lodge. Searching through the Jesuit Library, Lodge came across a manuscript which interested him. It was an example of the attempts of the missionaries to make formulas of the church accessible to the local Amerindians. Entitled "Doutrina Christãa na lingua Brasilica," it was a translation and adaptation of a primer into Guarani (pl. 6). This manuscript Lodge took with him and retained until his return to England. Long afterward he presented it to the University of Oxford, probably in gratitude for his incorporation as M.D. by the university in 1602, and added the inscription "Ex dono Thomae Lodge D.M. Oxoniensis, qui sua manu e brasilia deduxit." It is now MS Bodley 617 and is probably, except for the Cavendish manuscript and will, the only tangible relic of the voyage to survive. At Santos Lodge also got the idea for the story which he afterward claimed to have written while the ships were attempting to make their way through the Strait of Magellan. This was *A Margarite of America,* which he published in 1596. He also befriended an elderly Italian, Giuseppe Adorno, whose conversation he found scholarly; Adorno's daughter had married an Englishman, John Whithall, who had been largely instrumental in establishing earlier clandestine trading links with English seamen and merchants.[44]

Setting out at last, after too long a stay, the squadron sailed south for fourteen days with favorable winds, but on February 7 the wind began to blow hard. The storm was evidently a *pampero,* and Cavendish's decision to send some of the smaller vessels to take shelter in the Plate estuary was about the worst he could have taken. Riding into the teeth of the wind, the *Crow,* a 20-ton pinnace built at Santos, was lost with her crew, while the *Daintie,* laden with cargo and spoil from Santos, weathered the storm only to go for home.[45] The *Roebuck* lost both her boat known as a light horseman and her longboat, and the *Galleon Leicester* her longboat, while the loss of the boats and the reduction of the smaller ships to the *Black Pinnace* alone was to have very serious results for the expedition. The four remaining vessels were parted on the eighth and, surprisingly, no rendezvous had been appointed, so that the masters did not know

44. Lodge's Epistle to the Gentlemen Readers, prefixed to *A Margarite of America* (London, 1596), sig. [] 2v; Historical Manuscripts Commission, *Downshire Manuscripts* [ser. 75] (London), 2 (1938):93; Edward Andrews Tenney, *Thomas Lodge,* Cornell Studies in English, no. 26 (Ithaca, 1935), p. 117; C. H. Sisson, *Thomas Lodge and Other Elizabethans* (Cambridge, Mass.: Harvard University Press, 1933); James George, "Additional Materials on the Life of Thomas Lodge between 1604 and 1613," in *Papers Mainly Shakespearian,* ed. G. I. Duthie, Aberdeen University Studies, no. 147 (London, 1964), pp. 90–105.

45. If the *Daintie* did reach England her cargo, perhaps, provided some recompense to Davis for his losses and hardships: in *The seamans secrets* he makes no mention of her return.

where to run for. Davis, in the *Desire,* decided on Port Desire
(Deseado) and on his way he made contact with the *Roebuck* and
got her to accompany him. Cavendish was pressed hard by his men to
return to the comparative ease and comfort of Santos but he decided
to press on and, meeting with the *Black Pinnace,* entered Port Desire
(lat. 47° 46′ S, long. 65° 56′ W) with the *Galleon Leicester* on March
16, so that the squadron was once more reunited. The harbor was
scarcely suited to the larger vessels. Cavendish had to come ashore in
a boat hastily cobbled together and he soon took over the *Desire's*
longboat for his own use. With the return home of the *Daintie* it
looks as if some revision had been made in the plans for the voyage
and it is not unlikely that Davis was promised he would be allowed to
take the *Desire* with him in his search for the Northwest Passage
instead of his own ship, while Cavendish brought the two larger
ships to the Far East.

Conditions on the *Galleon Leicester* were by now very unhappy.
Cavendish tells us in his account of the voyage that the storms,
"whiche in deede I thincke to be such as worser mighte not be in-
dewred," had brought out the worst in his company, whom he
characterises as "the moste abiect mynded & mutanus Companye that
ever was Caried owt of Englande" (fol. 2r). Indeed such was the
atmosphere that Cavendish decided to leave the vessel and "tran-
shippe" to the *Desire,* where he found Randolph Cotton, the captain
of the *Daintie,* who had not accompanied his ship back to England.
By this time too the southern summer had gone and the passage of the
Strait in autumn weather was bound to present substantial difficulties.
Setting out as soon as possible, on March 20, the squadron made
good progress in rather heavy winds and rounded Cape Virgins
(Cabo Vírjenes) into the Strait of Magellan on April 8. For ten days
they worked forward steadily, reaching First Narrows on April 14
and crossing Philip Bay to Second Narrows by the sixteenth. Conditions became really difficult when they passed Cape Froward (lat.
53° 54′ S, long. 71° 18′ W) on April 18. The weather had now
become, as Cavendish said, "not durable for Christians" (fol. 3).
After rounding Cape Froward they were no longer able, on account,
as he tells us, of "the extremitie of stormes and the narrownes of the
straighte" (fol. 3) to run to windward any longer; so they took the
first shelter that offered, and somehow tucked themselves into a small
cove some four leagues west of Cape Froward on the south shore.
"This incredible stop," says Felix Reisenberg,[46] "at a narrow point in
the wildest part of the Strait, must have seemed like the end of the
world." In snow and frost, with their only longboat, seamen searched
the land round about for food, but they could find little but mussels,
"Fruits of the Countrey," "the barke of a tree that was like
Cinamon" (Winter's bark, *Cortex Winteranus* L.), and "Weeds of
the sea" to fill out their meager stores. These may have prevented
more of them from dying from scurvy. Cavendish tells us that on the
Galleon Leicester "in 7 or 8 daies in this extremitie there dyed ·40·
men and sickened ·70· so that there was not 50 men that were able
to stand vppon the hatches" (fol. 3). Others got frostbite, and
Anthony Knivet tells us he lost his toes and adds a good story that
"one Harris a Goldsmith lost his Nose: for going to blow it with his
fingers, cast it into the fire," though such extremes were unusual.

As May came in, it was clear that some drastic action must be
taken. Davis advised holding out, as the snow would soon pass and

46. *Cape Horn,* p. 124. On the location of Tobias Bay, as the place was named, see
fol. 3, n. 7, of transcription.

progress be possible again, and Jane says his men were ready to do this. Cavendish came to favor turning eastward. His argument was that, as they were bound for China, it was not of great consequence whether they reached it from one direction or another. It did matter very much to John Davis, however, as to proceed eastward would wreck his Northwest Passage plans. Cavendish went to visit the *Galleon Leicester,* his own ship, and put his case to the men for crossing the South Atlantic to the Cape of Good Hope. He knew the course and, he says, "I doubted not but soone to recover to this Cape where I shewed them I made noe doubte but wee shoulde releve our selffes, and performe to their Contentes our intended viage" (fol. 4). Raymond, Foxcroft, and Lancaster had set out for the East Indies by way of the Cape ahead of Cavendish and perhaps he hoped to catch up with Lancaster, who had, in fact, only cleared from Madagascar in February 1592. But, again, according to the manuscript, the men soon returned with a petition of their own, professing their loyalty to him as commander and proposing that since they were so short of provisions and equipment they should return to Brazil to refit. Cavendish tells us that he then took stock of the position. He had lost one suit of sails on the way out, and had no other in reserve, "for noe Shippes Carieth 3 neewe Shiftes of Sayles" (fol. 6), and the *Desire* was equally handicapped; all the ships were afflicted with rotting ropes and sails, cables had been lost, and victuals were extremely short. "I knewe well," he said, "that the wyndes were suche . . . as in two daies together we shoulde not be able to see 5 howers the place not a league over in breadeth." This being so, Cavendish says he agreed to accept the proposal to go back to Brazil, "which they so muche seemed to desire and I so much hated" (fol. 7). He says he would have preferred, if they went back, to have wintered at Puerto San Julián (lat. 49° 11' S, long. 67° 36' W), but this was a barred harbor which the larger ships could not enter, while Deseado lacked wood and water and had a poor anchorage. John Jane makes it clear that Davis expressed his continued disagreement, but the decision was taken and the squadron turned about, Cavendish returning to command the *Galleon Leicester*. It was at this point that, according to both Knivet and Jane, Cavendish put eight of the most seriously ill men on shore and left them to die. Whether or not they were moribund is not clear. Knivet, suffering from frostbite, was saved only, he says, by Captain John Cocke's intervention.

"Wee were beaten," says the manuscript, "owt of the Straighte with a moste monsterous storme at weste southe weste" (fol. 7). The ships kept together until May 20, when they were, according to Cavendish, at 47° S, near enough to the latitude of Port Desire, when the vessels parted in the night. On this crucial parting the stories are contradictory. Davis's was that Cavendish changed course during the night. John Jane indicates, as A. H. Markham says,[47] that the ships at nightfall were sailing close-hauled and due eastward. The *Desire*'s crew gave another explanation, implying that the ships were sailing almost into the wind (which was not possible), and that the *Galleon Leicester* cast about and the others sailed after her to the southeast. This Markham does not understand, but suggests that a change of tack, from the northwest toward the east, was intelligible in the evening, to keep from getting too close to the shore. Whatever went wrong, it seems strange that the *Galleon Leicester* and the

47. *The Voyages and Works of John Davis,* ed. A. H. Markham, Hakluyt Society, 1st ser., no. 59 (London, 1878), p. 104.

Roebuck went one way and the *Desire* and the *Black Pinnace* another. Once again the failure to arrange a rendezvous was to have serious consequences. Cavendish would accept none of the blame. He is quite unrestrained in his first reference to Davis—"that villaigne that hath bynn the death of mee and the decaie of the whole Accon . . . whose onely trecherie in Runinge from me hath bynn An vtter Ruyn of all" (fols. 1r–1v). He is more restrained but not less condemnatory later on (fols. 7–[7 *bis*]): "in the latitude of ·47· . . . Davys in the Desier and my Pinnis loste me in the night after which tyme I never hard of theme but as I synce vnderstode Davis his intention was ever to rune awaye. this is godes will That I shoulde put hym in truste that should be thend of my lief, and the decaye of the whole Action. for had not these two smale Shippes parted from vs we coulde not haue miscaried on the Coste of Brasele for the onelie decaye of vs was that wee could not get into theire barred harbors." He rightly guessed that the *Desire* and the *Black Pinnace* had gone back to Port Desire, but we may well ask why did he not search there as it would have meant only a short delay to return and make certain. Instead, he tells us, "the Roobucke and my self held our Course for Brasele & kepte togethere till wee Came to the latitude of 36," off the mouth of the Plate ([fol. 7 *bis*]), that is well over 700 miles north of Port Desire. The two vessels then encountered a storm, "the moste grevous storme that ever anye Christians indured vppon the seas to live" ([fol. 7 *bis*]). Knivet tells us that the *Roebuck* broke her mainmast and that afterwards they lost sight of her. We have from Knivet a graphic picture of Cavendish in action after this storm. Some of the sailors would not come up "to doe some business that was to bee done," so the "Generall," Cavendish himself, set about them "with the end of a Rope as bigge as mine arme," showing that conditions were still far from good and that Cavendish was resorting to violence to maintain some sort of ascendancy on board. But, "Now were wee all alone in a great ship," Knivet says, "and we knew not what wee were best to doe." The "best" was to loiter along the Brazilian coast for a fortnight and then make for Santos in the hope of finding some of their consorts, though nowhere are we told that firm arrangements had been made for a rendezvous there.

Meantime what of Davis? The *Desire* picked up the *Black Pinnace* in the morning but, he maintained, neither could sight the other ships. They cast about looking for them through the twenty-first and into the twenty-second, when a rising storm damaged them both, the *Desire* having the rigging of her mainmast broken and the *Pinnace* springing a leak. After some dissension—the master of the *Desire* urging them to sail on—it was resolved to put back to Port Desire. And this was done on May 26. They had some luck in doing so, for they found a more sheltered anchorage than they had known before, and also a pool of drinking water. But they were far from easy in their situation, with inadequate cables, rigging, and sails, and one boat only (the *Desire*'s having been taken by Cavendish some time before), and there being only a little pork and meal left of their original stores. They began setting up a forge to make bolts, spikes, and nails; they stripped part of a cable to make ropes; they repaired their rigging; and they collected many mussels and caught a large quantity of smelts. At this point discontent came into the open. There was a mutinous rising on both vessels. Davis and his master heard of its preparation and, managing to isolate two ringleaders, quelled it without violence. This episode makes it clear that many of the men suspected that Davis intended, with or without Cavendish, to make a

further attempt on the Strait, instead of awaiting his commander's
return or else following him to Brazil. Once Davis had established
his ascendancy, however, forty members of the company, headed by
himself and by Randolph Cotton, and including the two insurgent
leaders, Parker and Smith, signed a testimonial on June 2 proclaiming
their intention throughout to have been loyal to Cavendish and
declaring they would still either follow him or await his return. This
document gives a detailed account of the circumstances surrounding
the separation of the ships and the subsequent actions of the *Desire*
and the *Black Pinnace*. It agrees in general, but not in all details, with
that of John Jane, in whose narrative it is embedded. There is
scarcely enough evidence for a conclusive opinion to be given on the
available data, but it seems highly probable that Davis regarded
a return to Port Desire as the best way of achieving his own objectives
in the voyage, possibly arguing that if Cavendish was serious about
returning he would visit Port Desire in due course, while if he was
not, the remaining vessels were well rid of him. Cavendish himself,
even making allowance for his poor physical condition when he wrote
and the tendency toward self-pity which is evident in the narrative,
appears to have become at least hysterical and probably paranoic about
the supposed treachery and persecution of Davis. At the time it is
possible to sympathize in part with his feelings in attributing to
Davis's defection some, at least, of his misfortunes in Brazil.

Arriving back at that part of the Brazilian coast where he had been
on the outward journey,[48] namely at the Baia de São Vicente,
Cavendish yielded, he says, to the requests of his men to make a raid
on the nearby mainland primarily in order to seize some fresh food—
"his men dying with hunger," says the Jesuit John Vincent—as there
were some rich Portuguese farmsteads and a sugar mill nearby.
The first raid went very well even though the raiders had to go ashore
in a boat made of "sugar chests and barrell boards." The mill was
captured and also a large old boat, on which they managed to lade a
quantity of fresh food which was, says Knivet, "more welcome to us
than if it had beene gold," and so returned safely to the ship.
Cavendish had now a means, in this large boat, of carrying out a
search for his missing ships and so he sent her off to an island some
forty-five miles away to look for them. Meantime, the men were
anxious to continue their plundering ashore and on this occasion a
Brazilian Indian, who had accompanied them since their earlier visit
to Brazil, offered to act as a guide. Captain Barker was appointed to
command the shore party and was instructed to spend as little time on
land as possible and to return to the ship. Twenty-five men, including
Captain Edward Stafford[49] and Captain Southwell, who insisted on
going with Barker, were selected and they went off in the patched-up
boat. This was at dawn. In the afternoon the boat put back to the
ship with only a few men and with some maize, half a dozen hens
and a small hog. The smallness of this provision infuriated Cavendish, who sent the boat back with strict orders that the party was to
return. But there was no news of them until the next day. An Indian
was then seen signaling from the shore. Putting together a raft—for

48. References in Brazilian histories (e.g., F. A. Varnhagen, *História Geral do Brasil*,
ed. Rodolpho Garcia, 5th ed. [São Paulo, Ediçoes Melhoramentos, 1956], 2:45,
83–84) are brief and not very informative.
49. Captain Stafford's home was in the parish of St. Botolph's extra Aldersgate,
London. He appears to have been connected with the Gorges family through Sir
Robert Stafford (knighted 1545) who was the second husband of Jane Gorges,
Tristram's aunt. Frederick Brown, *Pedigree of Sir Ferdinando Gorges* (Boston,
1875), pp. 4–5.

they had now no boat—they took him off. He proved to be the Indian guide, wounded and with the worst possible news. The rest had been set upon, he said, by eighty Portuguese and three hundred Indians, and all, with their boat, had been killed or captured. Two or three only, John Vincent tells us, were left alive, "of whome one is a Japan boye." Cavendish tells us (fol. 10), "then I demaunded why the[y] came not a borde. the Indian answered me that some were vnwilling to Come and the Reste did nothing but eate hennes and hogges which they hadd there in aboundaunce and y^t they mynded nothing to Come aborde." Cavendish regretted very greatly that twenty-five of his best men should have thrown away their lives through disobeying orders. Until the large boat came back from the Ilha de São Sebastião (which is probably where she had been sent) the *Galleon Leicester* was virtually immobilized in the "River of Bertia," namely, the Canal de Bertioga. But the boat returned after eight days without news of the other vessels. However, when they least expected it, the *Roebuck* suddenly sailed across the mouth of the channel and, catching sight of the *Galleon Leicester,* fired a gun, to which the flagship replied and the vessels were soon reunited. Glad though Cavendish was to see the *Roebuck,* her condition proved, superficially at least, to be worse than that of his own ship. Though she still had her longboat, she had lost both mainmast and foremast in the storm and much of her canvas had gone, but she had, presumably, some reserves in her lockers, since she had been able to rig her mizzen.

Though it is likely that some repairs were undertaken, Cavendish's main preoccupation was revenge on the Portuguese. He decided that this could best be achieved by working both vessels up to Santos and, as he tells us, "to haue beaten hit to the ground" (fol. 11). Setting out to do so, he soon became aware that the channel was too shallow and that, without sufficient boats and pinnaces, the danger of going aground was too great—the *Galleon Leicester* indeed touched bottom before they turned back. An attempted attack by the Portuguese was beaten off and Cavendish had to limit his vengeance to a shore raid. Some eighty men embarked in the boats. They robbed a number of farms successfully and "gotte some quantitie of freshe vittaile" (fol. 12), or, as Knivet put it, "great store of Mandiora Roots [i.e., cassava], Potatoes, Plantons and Pineapples." Despairing of doing more damage, Cavendish resolved to make his way to an island some twenty leagues away, probably Ilha de São Sebastião, and there to do such refitting as was possible.

He had come to two conclusions of a drastic nature, both of which he kept secret or believed he had succeeded in so doing. The first was that it would be impossible to put both vessels in good order. He intended therefore to strip the *Roebuck,* the less reparable, and to transfer her usable equipment and stores, together with her crew, to the *Galleon Leicester,* and then to destroy her. The second was to pretend to his men that he intended to take both vessels away from Brazil to the island of St. Helena, where he could promise they would get food and water (since it was used as a port of call by the Portuguese East Indiamen) and where they might find rich galleons as prizes. In reality he intended—and there is no reason to doubt his sincerity on the point—once he had disposed of the *Roebuck* and refitted his own vessel so far as was possible, to slip away for the Strait although he knew that the men had sworn a compact among themselves never to return there and would probably mutiny. He decided, however, to postpone action for a time, though it is not unlikely that his intentions became known or, at least, suspected.

A Portuguese, who had been with them since they first reached the Brazilian coast, offered to pilot them to Espírito Santo—the modern Vitória on the Ilha de Espírito Santo (lat. 20° 19′ S, long. 40° 16′ W) —where, he said, the ships could pass over the bar. Cavendish now convinced himself that this place offered the only chance of obtaining adequate supplies of food. It took them eight days to sail north, and when they reached the harbor mouth the depth was found to be only an inadequate 15 to 17 feet instead of the 30 feet or more promised by the pilot. The bitter disappointment which Cavendish experienced was expressed by his turning in fury on the Portuguese. "The Generall," Knivet tells us, "without any triall caused him to be hanged, the which was done in a trice."

Yet all was not lost. Three ships could be seen lying off the town, and Cavendish decided that a surprise attack, if it could be launched at once, might turn the tide in their favor. Otherwise, the Portuguese might take precautions which would ruin their chances. But by now his influence over his men was slight. They would not obey him when he ordered an immediate attack, since they were "for the moste parte vtterlie vnwillinge to goe that nighte" (fol. 16). By the morning the Portuguese were ready. The narrow channel through which the attackers must proceed—"not a bove a burde Bolte shotte over" (fol. 18)—had been fortified on both sides, and the Portuguese, with their Indian allies, were in a position to ambush any English force which might attempt to make its way toward the town and the ships.

Cavendish tells in some detail of the misadventures which followed. He says he advised against an attack, as the Portuguese had fired a large part of the surrounding country, and the boats he had were inadequate to force a passage through the channel. Captain Morgan's job was to reconnoiter the approaches to the town, but not to land, and, if they were undefended, to cut out one or more of the enemy ships. Should a landing seem necessary and practicable, he was to come back to the ships and Cavendish would return to make it with a larger force. Morgan, by Cavendish's story, was dared by his men to land when the two Portuguese "sconces" or small forts, one on each side of the channel, were discovered. The *Roebuck*'s boat crew took the weakly defended entrenchments on the western side and held them against the boatloads of Portuguese who came out from the town, driving them back. Captain Morgan, with Cavendish's boat— the large one recently taken—with difficulty landed some men to attack the fort on the eastern side. But when they were ashore they were heavily attacked from a position of strength. Morgan and five others were killed, and a hail of arrows wounded most of those left in the boat, which pulled out into the channel leaving the rest of the landing party to be killed or captured. They then called across to their comrades on the other side to leave their entrenchments and to come and help. In their hurry to do so the *Roebuck*'s boat shipped water and the master put off from shore without his full complement. The remainder of his party, too, were thus left to the mercy of the Portuguese. The net result was that of the eighty men who set out only fifty-five got back to the ships and the majority of them were wounded, more or less severely. The effect of this on the *Galleon Leicester* was to cut down her effective complement to about fifty.

The next day the ships were unable to leave the bad roadstead for lack of wind, but Cavendish now planned to return southward again to the Ilha de São Sebastião, where at least they could get water and where they would decide what was to be done. Evidently, the plan to burn the *Roebuck* had got out, for that ship's company desired to go

home and in their own vessel—which was the view of the master, to
whom Cavendish had taken a violent dislike—he called him" a most
Cowardlie villaigne that euer was borne of a woman" (fol. 21).
Captain Cocke was now too sick to be of any use in guiding affairs,
and Cavendish tells us the *Roebuck* was scarcely sailable. All the sick
men, however, were on board the *Galleon Leicester* and both
surgeons on the *Roebuck* when they set sail. Also, the *Roebuck* had
three times the amount of food that the flagship had—if we can
accept Cavendish's account—and so, for forty-six men, had victuals
for one hundred and twenty for six months. Cavendish, as usual, does
not mince words about the *Roebuck*'s crew, whom he describes as
"these moste harde harted villaynes" who "determined that nighte
amongste them selues to lose me at there next convenient tyme the[y]
Could espye. & in this case To goe for Englande, leaveinge vs in the
moste greatest distres that euer one christian lefte a nothere" (fols.
24–25). His last word concerning the *Roebuck* is: "the next morninge
lokeinge for the Roobucke shee Coulde noe where be seene" (fol. 26).
One cannot blame the crew over much. The threat to burn the ship
and to transport them back to the Strait, by their ever hard-hearted
commander, was, understandably, too much for them.[50]

The large boat was the only one Cavendish now had left and she
was leaking so badly that he did not dare to use her to transport water
from the shore; so he kept to his original plan of sailing to the Ilha de
São Sebastião as rapidly as possible, leaving the *Roebuck* to her own
devices. There was just enough water left until the casks could be
refilled at the island. There the large boat was patched up for the
time being and made usable, but when Cavendish surveyed the ship's
resources it was clear that the condition of the cables, tackle, and sails
was now serious, both the sprit-sail and the fore-tops'l—"which two,"
said Cavendish, "the shippe moste principallye loueth" (fol. 27)—
being lacking and the remainder "more then half worne." As for
food, there were supplies for their ill and augmented company for
fourteen weeks only. While this depressed Cavendish it did not
unduly distress his men for, he tells us, they reckoned their position
was bad enough to force their commander to return to England, which
was now the best they hoped for. The health of the crew was
evidently improving, yet his appeals to their valor left them unmoved.
He urged them, he tells us, "that they would cheerefully goe
forewarde to atempte ether to make them selues famous in resalutelie
dyeinge, or in liveinge to performe that which wilbe to theire
perpetuall reputations" (fol. 27). Yet when he came into the open and
informed them he meant to proceed through the Strait he was met
with open defiance—"fourthewith they all with one consente affirmed
plainelie they woulde never goe that waye againe" (fol. 28).
Cavendish argued with them, saying that on their voyage they could
get and salt all the seals and birds they would need for food, while
the summer passage through the Strait was only six hundred leagues
compared with two thousand to England. Once they got through "wee
could not but make a moste riche viage" (fol. 28). This had little
effect, as he admits; only the master, Stephen Seaver, and the dying
Captain John Cocke, spoke up for his plan, so once again, Cavendish

---

50. The intercepted letter of John Vincent (alias Yates), referred to in n. 43 above,
assumed from what prisoners said that the *Roebuck* had been burned, saying, "Seigne
nowe that the water and earthe dyd fight agaynst him he burnt one of his sayles, for
lacke of maryners & mastes and went his wayes, wither no man knoweth with one only
whipped with the scourge of god for the Irreverence he comitted agaynst his divine
maiestie & his sayntes." For Vincent see Aubrey Gwynn, "The First Irish Priests in
the New World," *Studies* 21 (1932):213–38.

resorted to force. Seizing one of the ringleaders of the opposition by the shoulders he tied him up and threatened to strangle him with his own hands if there was any more resistance and, once more, the men capitulated in the face of their commander's passionate violence and agreed to accept his orders.

A first step in his plan was to turn the large boat into a seaworthy pinnace. For this purpose he brought her on shore, with his ship's carpenter and a guard of thirty soldiers and also, Knivet tells us, his cook, John Chambers, whose job it was to catch fish with a stake net he rigged up, as well as to cook them. The other healthy men were left on board to do such repairs to sails and rigging as was possible. What of the sick? Knivet says that he, with twenty others, was placed on shore, away from Cavendish's working party, and was left to live or die without attention. He himself was too ill to move but the others began foraging along the shore. They found "a kind of Pease" growing near the shore and ate a quantity of the beans, as a result of which they died. This was probably a bean containing poisonous quantities of cyanide. We may, however, doubt Knivet's claim that he was the sole survivor. His story of his own survival sounds incredible.[51] Somewhat revived by a rest on shore, hunger drove him to crawl along the beach collecting crabs and, finding a fire in a hollow tree, cooking them there. Thus refreshed, he worked his way further along the shore to where a whale had been driven ashore. On the half-rotten meat he recovered his strength and soon joined a further party of ailing men—some forty in all—also put on shore from the ship. These were evidently neither so helpless nor so unfortunate as the first party; indeed they seem to have been living in sufficient comfort for a number of the able-bodied men from the ship to join them, in spite of their orders to stay on board.

For twelve days, however, all went well enough with the working party. Substantial progress was made with the refitting of the large boat as a pinnace; planking, wood for fuel, and water casks were prepared. Sails were spread out for repair. Yet Cavendish remained, he tells us, uneasy. He feared treachery from his own men and surprise by the Portuguese. Before the *Roebuck* sailed away, he says that some Irishmen had made off with her boat in order to betray them to the Portuguese. Now, another Irishman, "a noble villaigne" (fol. 30), made a raft and got from the ship to the shore in order to incite the enemy to attack. The soldiers of his own guard were, he felt, scarcely more dependable and were quite liable to go over to the Portuguese. While there was something morbid about these fears, they were in some degree justified. The pinnace was well enough finished for Cavendish to bring her out to the ship and, it would appear, most of the shore party with her, but that night, before he had done anything to round up the unarmed men and the sick who were also on shore, the Portuguese and their Indian allies struck. The encampment of the sick men was attacked and twenty-eight out of thirty killed, Knivet and another man alone being taken prisoner. The fit men who were on shore were also unarmed, but they could and did run away so that Cavendish was able to take all but five of them off by boat the following morning, though he had to leave behind some firewood and water casks which had not been brought out to the ship and, worst of all, in his condition, a sail which had been spread out after repair.

In some ways the condition of the *Galleon Leicester* had improved.

51. Purchas, *Pilgrimes* 4 (1625): 1206–7.

Some fifty sick and wounded men had been disposed of and this
would almost have doubled the value of such provisions as they had.
The men that were left were mostly in fair health. Yet, though the
"great boat" was now a usable pinnace and many repairs had been
effected, the equipment and stores were still very inadequate for
an arduous voyage. In spite of this, Cavendish tells us, "I determined
with all possible speede to despatch & be gone for the straightes of
Magalane" (fol. 30). But their last misfortune, though minor in
comparison with earlier ones, had finally decided the crew: "for the
straightes," he tells us, "I could by noe meanes get my Companie to
giue their Consentes to goe" (fol. 32). Of the ninety men left, some
sixty were soldiers and, he admits, "all the men . . . were noe more
then able to waye our Ankors" (fol. 32). Cavendish himself was now
beginning to crack, but even so he did not wholly despair. He claims
to have told his men defiantly that he would still not agree to go
for England but would rather sink ship and crew together before he
would do so. Once again he regained some measure of ascendancy
over the men, who, he claims, "Vpon this . . . began to be more
tractable" (fol. 33), and proposed that, in the short run, they should
make for St. Helena, "And there ethere to make our selffes happie by
mending or endinge" (fol. 33). Food at least they were likely to find
there and perhaps a galleon from the Portuguese East Indies to make
them rich.

Cavendish's plan was to work along the coast until he could pick
up the southeasterly Brazilian current, which would enable him
to reach St. Helena (lat. 15° 56' S, long. 5° 42' W). He managed to
work from 29° to 20° S but at that point desired the men to turn
southward again as he was by now too far north to pick up the trade
winds. This they refused to do but, by some means, he bullied them
into taking the ship to 28° and turned north once more. As he came
within reach of the island he gave orders to steer at night east-north-
east. Instead, he claimed, the master steered northeast; thus they
missed St. Helena by, he says, 60 leagues. Finally, blown 18 leagues
to the west of the island, in the correct latitude, they were carried
away from it by the prevailing winds against which they could make
no headway. At this point Cavendish made a fresh survey of the
provisions on board and estimated that there was only enough left
for eight weeks' sailing. This was bad, though scarcely so bad as to
justify his statement that this was "As smale A portion, as euer men
were At in the seaes" (fol. 34). He pleaded with the crew, however,
to turn about and allow him to make a final attempt to reach St.
Helena, but now his ascendancy was gone and he had to accept their
decision to proceed northward, looking, unavailingly, for an island—
Ascension (lat. 7° 56' S, long. 14° 22' W)—placed on the charts in
8° S. What state of physical decline Cavendish had reached at this
time we cannot say, but, psychologically, he was far gone. The strain
of constantly asserting himself against his men and his ultimate
failure to make them obey him had destroyed, with his power of
command, his will to live. Moreover, his cousin, Captain John Cocke,
was dying and he expired when the ship was some 8° south of the
equator.[52] This was a final blow "amongst such hel houndes · my
spirit was Cleene spent" (fol. 35). Already he had decided, if they
reached Ascension "to haue there ended my vnfortunate lief" (fol.

52. On 29 May 1593 letters of administration of the estate of Captain John Cocke
of Prittlewell, Essex, who had died beyond the seas, were granted to Leonard Mathew
of Little Stanbridge, Essex. PRO, PROB 6/5, fol. 57v.

36). It sounds as if he had decided to commit suicide. When, finally, the island could not be found and the vessel turned northward for England at last Cavendish made up his mind he was dying and began to prepare systematically for death. We have no precise dates after the May parting but it is probable that the year was now well advanced: it was almost certainly October at least, and could have been November.

His Will and His Death

First Cavendish made his will.[53] This was, comparatively, a simple affair. Tristram Gorges was to be his executor and was to dispose of the *Roebuck* and the *Galleon Leicester* and all they contained should they both return. A hundred marks from the proceeds were to go to William Goodrich, one of the Queen's surgeons, and the rest, after the executor had paid his costs and recouped his own investment, to Anne Cavendish. By inference Cavendish did not intend the survivors on either vessel, whether sailors or soldiers, to get anything at all. If the *Desire* and the *Black Pinnace* returned, however, it was to be presumed that they might have a rich cargo on board. This was to be taken care of and realized. From this all adventurers were to have their shares; the *Desire* was to go to Sir George Carey, together with a quarter of Cavendish's share in her lading, and the residue to Anne. The witnesses were Thomas Hammond, who has not been identified; Stephen Sever or Seaver, who had been in command of the *Roebuck* in 1590 and was the master of the *Galleon Leicester* on this voyage, and Robert Hues, the mathematician and geographer who had accompanied Cavendish in the circumnavigation.

Much more elaborate was the document he began to pen for Tristram Gorges, the original of which has for so long lain unread and uncommented on. As we have seen, it is written firmly and evenly throughout. Even when, on the thirty-fifth page (fol. 32) he writes, "but nowe I am growne so weake & fainte as I am scarce able to holde the penn in my hande," the writing does not falter. Nor does the vigor and strength of the narrative weaken until he comes to the death of Captain Cocke, when the story trails off into despair. Whatever conclusions we may come to about Cavendish's judgment on the voyage, or whatever we may decide his mental state was when he wrote, it cannot be denied that he gives a forthright and lucid statement of the causes of the failure of his expedition as he, through the anguish of disappointment and sickness, saw them. He almost breaks down when he writes "& now consider wheth[er] a harte made of fleshe be able to indure so manye misfortunes, all faleinge vppon me withowt Intermission, I thancke my god that in endinge of me he hath pleased to Ridde me of all furder troble & misshappes" (fol. 36). Yet he is able to continue clearly with his instructions to Gorges, until, just before his final commendation of himself to his friends, he says, "beare with this scribleinge for I protest I am scante able to holde A penne in my hand" (fol. 38).

Purchas omitted some details of the business arrangements in the will. Some other matters were omitted by him also as being too private and personal, perhaps reflecting on persons, such as Sir Carew Ralegh, who were still alive when *Pilgrimes* was being prepared for press. From the details we can make certain inferences, for example, Cavendish's complete reliance on his executor, Tristram Gorges of

53. See p. 128 below.

Budockshed, near Plymouth, for whom he retained the warmest feelings of friendship, as he did toward Sir George Carey, governor of the Isle of Wight, one of his principal backers. Then we have Cavendish's pointed comments on his creditors and fellow adventurers, with whom he expects Gorges to deal at as little cost as possible. For John Davis, he reserves only malice and expresses the hope that, if Davis gets home, Gorges will see that "hee of all others maye repe leaste gayne" (fol. 1v). As for Carew Ralegh, a bond of £200 was payable to him, "which," Cavendish says, "he will infinitli troble you for." Gorges is told, "you knowe his humor[,] he onelie likes to bargayne[,] satisfie hym in the same sorte" (fol. 1v). A bond for £250 to two London merchants, he is told, "you maye sleightlie Compounde for" (fol. 1v). On the other hand, besides what he may get by the will, Sir George Carey is to have his four iron guns back, together with two brass demi-culverins from the *Roebuck* "with myne Armes on them." Sir Henry Palmer is to be paid his £20 owing. For his bill of adventure for £300, Gorges is told, Henry Seckford can claim only as a part-victualer, but is warned, "he is an hungrye man and one that will seeke muche, vse your discretion with hym" (fol. 2r), though later he advised Gorges to put him in as an additional executor if he wanted help on the business side. A few other creditors are remembered near the end of the document: Richard Cocke, brother of the dead Captain John, a customs official at Southampton, and a man called Elliot. Finally, Gorges is told that the document was for his private use and should be shown to Sir George Carey alone. Earlier, Cavendish had said that he had appointed "some of the moste sensibleste men . . . to make discourse vnto you of all these accidentes" (fol. 1r). He does not name them, but they are not unlikely to have included one or more of the three witnesses to his will. Unfortunately no narrative by any of those who accompanied him to the end has survived. The individual who brought the packet containing the will and the last letter to Gorges was to receive from him the substantial reward of £40.

This was the last thing that is known of Thomas Cavendish. When he died and where, precisely, in the ocean waters he was buried we do not and probably shall never know. He had a long run of ill luck. He was not as well equipped as he should have been for such a long voyage. Clearly, the *Galleon Leicester,* for all the strength she might have provided in Far Eastern waters, was a mistake. Her size, her unwieldiness, the large, unruly, and heterogeneous company, were all against her. Deprived of boats and pinnaces she became almost useless for coastal work, and she was barely manageable at sea. The men doubtlessly included many on whom little reliance could be placed. There is no evidence that Cavendish was a coward in this last voyage. There is sufficient evidence that he was a bully and, perhaps, enough to say that he was savagely inhumane in abandoning his sick and injured men on shore—though there may have been mitigating circumstances. That he lost his temper easily and stalked about in tremendous rages, when nobody near him was safe, cannot be doubted. That this showed his capacity for effective leadership cannot be confidently argued, even though, until almost the end, he did succeed in pushing his men along the course he himself decided. He does not seem to have displayed any ability to seek for or to take advice. For a man who had brought the *Desire* around the globe with such credit he was shaky in his judgments. His decisions to attempt passage of the Strait of Magellan at the approach of winter shows a foolhardy recklessness or an insensitiveness to maritime conditions

unexpected in one of his experience. His tenacity may be praised
yet it cannot be said his determination to go on when going on
seemed a fantastic impossibility to everyone else on board the *Galleon
Leicester* argued good sense. His determination to destroy his ship,
his men, and himself rather than return to England was either the
attitude of a man blinded by romantic heroics or that of someone
fundamentally unstable. There can be little doubt that he was at least
a little mad well before the end. Though it is dangerous to read too
much into the last document he wrote, there is sufficient corroboration
from Knivet and John Jane to indicate that Cavendish was obsessed
with the feelings of persecution which he sustained, as he thought, at
the hands of his men at all stages in the voyage. Always there was
an enemy working against him; always there were plots. Faults were
never accidents or mistakes but always deliberate attempts to thwart
him or ruin his purpose. Always, almost everyone was wrong except
himself. An able leader in such circumstances as the Elizabethan
voyagers found themselves had to be something of an egotist, but he
did not need to be the complete egotist Cavendish makes himself out
to be. It is impossible to escape the conclusion that his symptoms
were paranoic and that they mounted before the end over the edge
of insanity.

His determination, doubtless born of pride as well as instability,
never to return to England, and his men's determination, victorious
only at the bitter end, never to go back to the Strait, makes a dramatic
conflict of the latter part of the voyage. It is one which cannot be
described as other than a tragedy, and it was strange indeed that no
playwright read it as such. But it was blacker, earlier at least, in his
own mind than it was in reality. The deepening gloom that spread
over him, and the wish for death that went with it, made Cavendish
magnify the perils, great as they were, which afflicted his ship and her
consorts. It is an ironic commentary that in the end not only the
Galleon Leicester but the *Roebuck* and the *Desire* herself survived
and made their voyage safely home, even though the *Desire* had only
a handful of her complement alive.

The story of the *Galleon Leicester* after Cavendish's manuscript
ends is so far not known. But it is likely that the ship obtained food
and water and, probably, sails and tackle as well, not too long after
the death of her commander. As we do not know her longitude when
she was at approximately 8° north latitude it is impossible to tell
whether she made her way back to South America or into the West
Indies, making use of the equatorial current, or whether she reached
some of the Atlantic islands. The least unlikely place for her to have
made for was the Azores, since there she could be virtually certain
of meeting with English privateers and might also obtain some
supplies on shore. It is even possible that there or elsewhere she
picked up a prize or two so that she limped home not only more or
less intact but with some profit. Or, it may be that enough men died
or went short to bring her direct to England with the meager supplies
she had when Cavendish wrote. Similar conjectures would cover the
case of the *Roebuck* except that her lack of masts and sails was such,
at least in Cavendish's opinion, that some means of supplying these
must have been found. In her case the possibility that she took a
prize off the Brazilian coast is substantial, and such an encounter
would have given her all she required in the way of equipment and
could, too, have provided some profit. It is even conceivable, since
both ships were together in Portsmouth in March 1593, when they
are first heard of again, that they met with each other off the Azores

and sailed home together. The return of the two principal vessels may then have been neither so tragic (in spite of the loss of their commander) nor even so unprofitable as it might well have been expected to be.

We are much better informed about the fate of the *Desire* and the *Pinnace*. It was, indeed, much more pitiable, just as their achievement was so much the more to be admired. John Davis was at least as tenacious of his purpose as Cavendish, but he was tougher in body and mind and more capable in practical matters. In John Jane's narrative we can follow his progress from June 1592 onward. Over two months were spent at Port Desire in refitting the ships and salting seals until, finally, on August 7, the two vessels were ready to set out for the Strait. Sighting the Falklands on the fourteenth, they made Cape Virgins on the eighteenth and entered the Strait. They made excellent progress and, by the twenty-fifth, "we ankored," says Jane, "in a good coove, within fourteene leagues of the South sea" —that is, in one of the inlets on the south side of Sea Reach. They there proposed to wait for a time for Cavendish, but this was a mistake, perhaps a fatal one, since the winter had not yet gone and steady winds were the exception rather than the rule. Soon the extreme cold, for which the men were not prepared, began to take its toll. A number of them died, while the salted seals went bad. Davis was forced to attempt to go on. On September 13 they set out, hoping to reach the island of Santa Maria (lat. 37° S, long 73° 30' W), south of Valdivia. This had been a tentative rendezvous on their previous attempt, and Cavendish was likely to call there if he was still following. But now design was one thing, execution another. The fierce spring winds were dead contrary so that the vessels were twice driven back from the open sea. Eventually they managed to put back into the Strait, but they lost one of the *Desire*'s two remaining cables and had to moor her to trees growing on the shore. During an interval of lighter winds they were able to make a few emergency repairs to the *Desire* and to the *Black Pinnace,* which had so far kept up with the larger ship very well. The men had been resolute so far, but now they were divided on going forward or back. Davis persuaded them— and it is characteristic of him that where Cavendish would have driven, he could lead—that going on was not just a matter of the "blind affection that we bare the General," but offered the best hope of relief and even survival. Thus it was decided to make a further attempt on the passage and, on October 2, both vessels passed Cape Pilar out of the Strait of Magellan and thus "put into the South Sea and were free of all land." At this moment, however, a gale from the west-northwest sprang up, and by October 4 both vessels were in a bad way, so much so that Davis despaired of keeping enough canvas and rigging in working order to enable him to survive and did not dare turn back. On the night of the fourth the *Black Pinnace* disappeared, and there is little doubt she foundered with all hands. Davis hung on tenaciously until October 10, hoping every hour that the winds would slacken or change. When they did so he was nearly at the end of his tether, but he succeeded in reentering the channel after narrowly escaping being wrecked on Cape Deseado. Once they were in the Strait again, the wind turned favorable and they raced through until they were able to put into a cove some seventy-five miles from Cape Pilar. Here they were able to refresh themselves a little, though food was short. When they set out again navigation proved very difficult as the ship was not sailing well. Davis's chart, however, which he had made as he sailed through the Strait with

Cavendish, proved invaluable, so that he passed Cape Virgins on the twenty-seventh and reached the Isla de Pingüino, alongside Port Desire, on October 30.

On the islands, now in late spring, there were masses of Magellanic penguins, seals, and seabirds of all sorts so that the *Desire's* immediate wants, in food at least, could be supplied. Davis put his ship on shore so that she could be scraped and repaired, and had his boat ferry backward and forward to the island to fetch food. A group of men—including most of the leaders of the previous mutiny who were still on somewhat edgy terms with Davis—decided to make a shore excursion. The boat landed them on the mainland on its way back from the islands and they set out to walk to the ship in hopes of finding deer and "ostriches" (rheas). They were attacked by a body of Patagonian Indians and nine of them were killed. Jane, and apparently Davis also, regarded this tragedy as a judgment on them for their past misdeeds. One of Davis's major problems, now, was to preserve the food which was available in such great quantities. He managed to make a little salt, which was used for preserving, but the bulk of the penguins taken, 20,000 in all, were dried, since the weather was now warm. Equally important, they managed to get quantities of scurvy grass, which would give them at least temporary immunity from scurvy.

The tides were very high during the latter half of December and the *Desire* was not very easy to load; it was so difficult in fact that Davis finally decided to cast off although there were still some 6,000 dried penguins on shore. On December 22 they set out for England, Davis now recognizing that his ship was not fit to enter the Pacific, while it was clear that they had finally lost touch with Cavendish. The voyage up the coast of South America was rapid and uneventful and they reached the island of Placentia (Ilha Grande, lat. 23° 17′ S, long. 44° 29′ W) on 30 January 1593, some three months after Cavendish had finally left the coast of Brazil. Their main need now was water, and casks to put it in. They were fortunate, they thought, in finding the island deserted by the Portuguese, and they went ashore to find in the old gardens there cassava and other vegetables, which must have been a welcome relief from their staple diet of penguin meat. However, the men proved too unsuspicious and had only got 8 tuns of water on board before they were surprised by a large force of Portuguese and Indians who came across from the mainland. Out of twenty-three, only two escaped and one was made prisoner, the remainder being killed.[54] The survivors managed to reach the ship and warn Davis so that he was able to get the *Desire* hurriedly to sea and to escape from two pinnaces which put out from Rio de Janeiro to intercept him.

The main problems now were that, with only twenty-seven men left, there was scarcely sufficient crew to work the ship and, further, water was very short. Contrary winds held them back for a time off Cape Frio and they suffered for lack of water, but their luck turned again when the winds changed, rain fell, and they began to make rapid progress. But soon a new danger threatened. In the equatorial heat the penguins, probably inadequately dried in any case, went rotten, and soon the ship was crawling with maggots which proved so voracious that nothing was safe from them—"there was nothing

---

54. The episode is briefly described (from the Portuguese side) by a Spaniard, Martín del Barco Centenara, *Argentina y Conquista del Río de la Plata* (Lisbon, 1602), fol. 228.

that they did not devour, only yron excepted," says John Jane. And
following on this, disease appeared. Certainly some of the men
afflicted had scurvy, though there may have been a skin infection from
the carrion as well. The sick were in great misery as the vessel worked
slowly northward and, gradually, one after another, died, eleven in
all. Of the sixteen that remained only five stayed at all healthy, among
them Captain Davis himself, and on them lay the burden of working
the ship. At long last, land, Irish land, was seen and the handful
of survivors managed to bring the ship into Berehaven, County Cork,
on 11 June 1593, without as Jane says, "victuals, sailes, men, or any
furniture." Local men managed to help them to bring the ship to a
mooring and there Davis left her in charge of the master while he
and a few others set out in an English fishing boat on the sixteenth
for Padstow. For the *Desire* the outcome of the voyage was bare
survival, but Davis was at least spared to defend his honor against
Cavendish's charges and to sail another day.

   Cavendish's last voyage was not one of the great achievements of
the Elizabethan seamen, but it is easy to underestimate its interest.
It illustrates very well many of the problems of carrying through a
long-distance expedition by sea, the difficulties of maintaining effective contact between the different vessels of a squadron, of disciplin-
ing and feeding a mixed company of soldier-adventurers and seamen,
of making raids on Spanish-Portuguese colonies which would supply
those wants that the ships' stores could not, or did not, furnish so
as to make them fully effective at sea. The fact that in most of the
encounters in Brazil, except the sack of Santos, the local settlers and
their Indian slaves and allies were successful, was partly a matter of
luck, but it also reflects the need for a greater vigilance than was
maintained by either Cavendish or Davis. The only piece of discovery
which the expedition carried through was a more thorough exploration of the Strait of Magellan than had hitherto been made by
Englishmen. Cavendish had mapped the Strait well in 1587, but there
is little doubt that Davis's chart, of which John Jane speaks but which
has not survived, would have represented a considerable improve-
ment on the Cavendish map. The bitter experiences which the ships
had, in failing to make their way out of the Strait either in winter or
in the spring, no doubt played their part in building up the story
of the horrors of the entry to the not-so-pacific ocean. If we leave the
Daintie out of account, and regard the loss of the *Crow* and of the
Black Pinnace as not unduly heavy, we are left with the fact that only
about one hundred men came back in the three principal vessels. At
least two hundred of the original complement, and possibly appre-
ciably more, had perished. This heavy mortality is characteristic of
most of the longer voyages of the period through tropical waters, but
it suggests that one chief defect of Cavendish's expedition was that
it was both too large and somewhat too heavily manned, while the
vessels seem to have been unusually and unduly dependent on
one another. The greatest English voyages were carried through by
one or two vessels lightly manned. Drake, in his circumnavigation,
took immense pains to prepare food and drink for a long voyage, and
he and Richard Hawkins alike had some conception of effective antiscorbutic measures, but little of this foresight was shown, as far as we
can tell, by Cavendish. Perhaps he was too fortunate in the 1586–88
voyage, mistaking luck for skill, so that he took much less care than
he should when preparing for that of 1591. To Dr. K. R. Andrews,
Cavendish's failure in 1591–92 was a just reward for the amateurish
carelessness of his preparations, and his weaknesses as a leader

when put to the test.[55] Yet in the end the human interest of the voyage is uppermost. It lives in the competent narrative of John Jane and the vivid ramblings of Anthony Knivet, but, most of all, in the manuscript which Thomas Cavendish himself wrote during the bitter struggles of his penultimate days of life.

The Aftermath of the Voyage

The aftermath of the voyage makes a somewhat complicated story in which there are still a number of loose ends. It begins with the grant of letters of administration in the Prerogative Court of Canterbury of the estate of Thomas Candishe of the parish of St. Anne, Black-friars, to Anne Dudley, alias Caundish, his natural sister, on 14 March 1593[56] This provides the first evidence that the *Galleon Leicester* and the *Roebuck* were back in England with news of Cavendish's death. Whether the ships returned separately or together, they both put into Portsmouth and this may have been the arrangement at the departure of the squadron in 1591. Whether this was done because Sir George Carey, established nearby on the Isle of Wight, was prominently associated with the expedition or whether Cavendish had a number of backers in the town—of which he had, as we have seen, been made an honorary freeman on 9 September 1590—is not clear. The Privy Council sent a letter on 18 March 1593[57] to the mayor and officers of Portsmouth to inform them that Robert Dudley (as Anne's husband) had taken out letters of administration for the goods of Thomas Cavendish "latelie deceased at the seas" and that he should receive their help. Dudley was the son of the late Earl of Leicester by Lady Sheffield but was never able, in spite of much litigation, to establish his legitimacy. He had fallen in love with and married, secretly, Cavendish's sister Anne, possibly before the expedition sailed in 1591. Since the queen, to whom Anne was then a maid of honor, regarded any assault, honorable or otherwise, on the virginity of her attendants as almost treasonable, Dudley had done something to which considerable risks were attached, and, indeed, in October 1591 we learn that "Master Dudley is forbidden the Court for kissing Mistress Candishe in the presence, being his wife as it said."[58] Dudley seems to have made his peace with the Queen by 1593 and he was now to act, as he thought, as the administrator of his brother-in-law's effects. However, it is probable that already by the time the Privy Council sent out the instructions, one of the survivors on board the *Galleon Leicester,* not improbably one of the three witnesses to the will, Thomas Hammond, Stephen Seaver, or Robert Hues, had brought to Tristram Gorges what we have seen described (see p. 6) as "a wrightinge written with his owne hande sealed vpp by master Thomas Caundishe in a Certaine Packett with his will . . . sealed vpp" and had duly received his reward of £40. Gorges stepped in at once as executor, acting in person or through an agent with some speed and determination in order to prevent the dissipation of whatever might have been brought back on board the *Galleon Leicester* and the *Roebuck.* The adventurers and sailors who had suffered so much hardship found themselves, at least in some cases, deprived of any reward for their labors. All who sailed on such an expedition

55. Kenneth R. Andrews, *Elizabethan Privateering* (Cambridge: Cambridge University Press, 1964), pp. 69–70.
56. PRO, Prerogative Court of Canterbury, Administrations Act Book, 1592–98, PROB 10/5, fol. 49.
57. *Acts of the Privy Council, 1592–93* (London, 1901), pp. 122–25.
58. Historical Manuscripts Commission, *Cecil MSS* [*ser.* 9], 4 (London, 1892):153.

as Cavendish's were entitled to their shares of spoil taken at sea, while those who had invested as well in the victualing or fitting out of the vessels shared in the gross proceeds of the expedition. On May 14 the Privy Council intervened[59] on behalf of some of these men. Tristram Gorges was sent a stiff letter informing him that twelve men who had returned on the *Galleon Leicester*—the four named being John Theobald, Robert Russel, William Harrison, and Gabriel North, and all of them men who had previously served the Queen well in the Netherlands as soldiers—had complained. As a result Gorges was told he must not deny them "their partes and shares of such goodes, ordinaunce and spoile as by their endeavour and valour was obteyned and brought home in the ship called the Gallion Leycester." It is likely therefore that Gorges, acting at least partly in the interests of Anne Dudley as the principal beneficiary under the will, was busy rapidly realizing some assets from the returned vessels.

What, precisely, was brought back is not, at present, known. It is highly probable that a certain amount of valuable property was taken in the surprise and sack of Santos on the way out and that this had been retained throughout the tribulations the vessels had suffered, while the less unsuccessful shore raids on the return voyage may well have produced some portable wealth as well as a little badly needed food. Whether either or both ships made their way back to the Brazilian coast after our narrative ends and obtained further spoil there, or even sugar and dyewoods by legitimate trade, cannot so far be ascertained. Similarly, too, they may have picked up a prize or prizes in the vicinity of the Azores on the way home. Whatever it was it was small compensation for the losses and dangers suffered by the men who returned and they clearly earned their shares, whatever their late commander may have thought of them, individually and collectively, at various stages in the voyage.

By the beginning of July the Privy Council had had its attention drawn to another matter arising out of "letters received from Master Thomas Cavendyshe." These could have been additional letters in the packet mentioned above of which we have no further knowledge, but it is almost certain that Tristram Gorges, in order to establish his authority to deal with Cavendish's possessions, had had to produce Cavendish's narrative and charge to him—confidential though it was —and that this, with the will, made up the "letters" referred to. It appears that the manuscript was retained for a time by the council. On July 1 a group of high officials in Devon and Cornwall—Sir William Courtenay, Sir Francis Godolphin, Edward Seymour, George Carey, and Sir Francis Drake—were told[60] that, on the basis of these letters and other probable conjectures, two of the vessels in Cavendish's expedition, the *Desire* and the *Black Pinnace,* were believed to have "passed through the Streightes of Magelen into the South Sea, where prizes of greate value and riches are often-tymes taken." Should these vessels come to land they were to be taken over by the local authorities so that the crews might not get away with any of their contents and so that "the owners and adventurers maie take order for the safetie of the goods." Hatches were to be nailed down and an inventory made of anything found either in the cabins or above the hatches, while the crews were to be examined on the results of their voyage. The irony of these preparations can best be appreciated by considering the fate of the vessels. The *Black Pinnace* was gone forever, and the

59. *Acts of the Privy Council, 1592–1593,* pp. 231–32.
60. Ibid., pp. 345–47.

Desire, so far from bearing home the riches of the Pacific shores or of Asia, had been barely able to limp into Berehaven with a handful of men on June 11 and had probably not yet been able to make her way to an English port.

It is clear too that, besides alerting the Privy Council to the possibilities of John Davis's returning with a rich cargo, Cavendish's last letter to Gorges had also strongly prejudiced the council against him, and he was presumed to be a treacherous and dangerous character. Davis, taking passage on an English vessel from Berehaven on June 16, is likely to have reached Padstow about the eighteenth and from there he must have gone to his house at Sandridge, near Dartmouth, and so it is not unlikely that he was at home by the time the letter of July 1 was dispatched from London. This was followed up by a further letter[61] from the Privy Council to Drake and the rest, dated July 9, instructing them to arrest one "Captain Davies," who was said to have "lately aryved at Dartmouthe or thereabouts," while, on July 30, Bryan Chamberlain, one of the messengers of the council, was ordered to bring Davis to London.[62] Thus it was in custody that John Davis, after all his trials and sufferings, came back to the capital. We have no record of his interrogation. There is little doubt, however, that he was confronted with Cavendish's charges, and it is evident that he was not found guilty of deserting his commander, though it appears that he was bound over to appear again if called upon to answer further charges if they should be made. The Privy Council registers are lacking from 26 August 1593, but it may well be that he was examined in the High Court of Admiralty as well as by the Privy Council and that some record of his interrogation may, eventually, be found. He was able to embark not long after on his important book, *The seamans secrets,* to which he prefixed, from Sandridge on 20 August 1594, a dedicatory epistle to the Lord High Admiral, Lord Howard of Effingham. In this he makes an attempt to exculpate himself publicly from the charges preferred against him by Cavendish, though in sorrow rather than in anger against his late commander, who "was content," he said, "to account me to be the authour of his ouerthrow, and to write with his dying hand that I ranne frome him, when that his owne Shippe was returned many moneths before me."

One result of this aftermath of the voyage was to delay the proving of Cavendish's will, probate on which was not finally granted until 4 February 1596. We have no direct evidence for the reasons behind this long delay, but it may have ensued from the withholding of Cavendish's last letter, and even the holograph will itself, by the Privy Council until Thomas Cavendish's charges against Davis and others had been finally disposed of. The will was eventually brought before the Prerogative Court of Canterbury by Tristram Gorges, where his legal representative, Walter Clerke, produced for the court the notes entitled "A Remembraunce" which we have already mentioned, a discreetly edited selection of passages from the manuscript[63] which is worth some discussion in detail.

The first point of interest is that Cavendish's own manuscript still bears some physical signs of an examination which was evidently made for the purpose of compiling the selection; indeed it is hard to see what other purpose the drawing of a hand as an indicator which appears in the margins on several pages can have had. The first passage in the selection is not, however, marked in the manuscript by

61. Ibid., p. 375.
62. Ibid., p. 435.
63. See pp. 148–49 below.

a hand. It comes from folio 1r, and reads: "I have made a simple will wherein I have made yo^u sole and onelie disposer of all such little which is lefte./ The Roe Bucke lefte me in the most desolatest case that ever man was lefte in [:] what is become of her I cannot ymagyne / But yf she be reterned into Englande it is a most admirable matter / But yf she be att home or anie other my goodes whatsoeuer reterne into Englande I haue made yo^u onelie possessor of them." This agrees (except in spelling) with the manuscript. The first passage in the manuscript to have a hand in the margin is that at the top of folio 36, where Cavendish declares that he would have committed suicide had he reached the island of Ascension ("meaneinge if I had found hit to haue there ended my vnfortunate lief"). This is not in the selection, however, but a passage on the same page (line 14), which also has a hand in the margin is there—"And nowe to retorne to our private matters I have made a will wherein I have geven specyall charge that all goodes whatsoever belongeth to me to be delivered into your hands. For goddes sake refuse not to doe this last request for me." This, too, agrees in meaning with the manuscript except that "belonges" has become "belongeth."

The third passage in the summary comes from folio 37, lines 10–29, in the manuscript, where there is a hand both at line 18 and at line 26. It reads: "I have geven Sir George Carey the Desire yf ever she retorne for I alwaies promised hym her yf she retorned and a little parte of her gettinge yf anie suche thinge happen [.] I praye yo^u see y^t performed/ To vse complementes of love nowe att my last breath were frivolous but knowe, that I lefte none in England whome I loved halfe so well as your selfe, whiche yo^u in suche sorte deserved att my handes as I can by noe meanes requite / I have lefte all that little remaynynge unto yo^u not to be Accomptable for anie thinge. That which yo^u will yf yo^u fynde anie Overplus of Remaynder your selfe speciallie beinge satisfyed to your owne desire I gave vnto my sister Ann Caundishe [.] I have wrytten to noe man livinge but yor selfe, leaving all friends and kinsmen, onlie reputinge yo^u as deerest." Some textual points of interest emerge from this passage. The ends of several lines in the manuscript have now gone. Line 23 has "Remayn[ ]," the summary "Remaynder" and Purchas "remayned." Line 25 ends with "sister" and part of a letter or letters beginning the last word which could be part of "A," where the summary has "Ann" and Purchas "Anne." Line 26 has "ma[ ]," the summary and Purchas "man." Lines 27–28 read in the manuscript "but your self, leveinge all frindes an[d] kynsmen onelie reputeinge you as [ ]," while the summary has "but your selfe, leaving all friends and kinsmen, onely reputing you as dearest," with the sense of which Purchas agrees.

The final group of passages in the summary forms a patchwork from folio 38, the last page of the manuscript. The latter has a hand by the passage on lines 1–3 where Cavendish instructs Gorges to give "the Copie of my vnhappie proceedeinges in this action" only to Sir George Carey, but the summary starts with lines 13–16, "I haue noe more to saie, but take this last farewell that yo^u haue lost the Lovingest freinde that was lefte by anie," and continues with lines 17–19. "Noe more but as yo^u love god doe not refuse to vndertake this last request of myne." The summary omits the commendation to Gorges's wife in line 16 and the passage about being unable to write further in line 23 and gives the concluding words, which are in the manuscript only, not in Purchas. From the right-hand side of the bracket the summary has "By hym that most loved yo^u Thomas

Caundyshe," where the manuscript has "By him that [   ] loved you. Thomas C [   ]," and it concludes with the words from the left-hand side—"I praye yo^u cause to be delivered to the Bearer thereof Fortie Powndes / Tho Caundyshe"—which agree with the manuscript.

The value of this detail is to show that the summary is authentic and that it even adds a few words to the text of the manuscript and to Purchas, but it reveals also something of the emphasis behind the selection on the part of Gorges. In the first place the selection emphasizes Cavendish's outstanding affection for Tristram Gorges— indeed it appears almost fulsome in this respect though this is not at all so obvious when the passages are read in their context. In the second place the selection stresses the extent of Gorges's discretion to dispose of whatever property was left after he and Sir George Carey were satisfied. Anne was to get the remainder, but only after Gorges had decided whether anything should remain. Affection for Cavendish's sister is not, indeed, expressed. Finally, there is a certain amount of suppression, as where Gorges omits mention of the suggestion Cavendish made that Henry Seckford might be joined as his co-executor. The selection was, in effect, an *ex parte* statement of Gorges's case before the Prerogative Court that he should be left in unfettered control of whatever Cavendish had left. Yet its acceptance by the court as a codicil to the will in the final sentence gave it equal authority with the holograph will itself. The decree of the court was duly attached to the will and the whole documentation entered in its register.

It is clear from the decree that Anne Dudley had tried to maintain her position as administratrix against the actions of Tristram Gorges as executor, but judgment was given against her and sole authority was given to Gorges, the summary being accepted as a legitimate gloss on the holograph will and as supporting evidence of its authenticity. A novel feature was the appearance of a third party intervening, namely, another sister, Beatrix Denys, who had married Thomas Denny or Denys.[64] She too was denied any interest in the disposal of Thomas Cavendish's estate. It is difficult for us to know whether there was sufficient cause for this protracted litigation. The will said that Anne Dudley was to have the residue of the estate. Gorges was not to have anything for himself, so far as we can see, whether he or Anne Dudley should be finally recognized as executor. The point at issue was that if Anne succeeded in retaining her executorship under the first grant of administration in 1593 she would have had much more freedom in disposing of the assets than if she was to receive what was left only after Gorges had looked after the interests of Sir George Carey and other persons mentioned not only in the will but in the manuscript it accompanied. A factor, too, in Gorges's persistence is likely to have been his feeling that he was bound in honor to carry out the wishes of his friend so strongly and movingly conveyed to him.

It may be worthwhile looking at Cavendish's costs and the potential of his residual estate, even though we know little about either from direct evidence. It is indeed possible that some appraisement of the ships which returned may yet be found in the voluminous records of the High Court of Admiralty or that the inventory which would have been compiled of his surviving material possessions when

---

64. This is confirmed by Thomas Denny's statement in 1604, "I married the sister of Sir Robert Dudley his first wife." *The Voyage of Robert Dudley to the West Indies, 1594–1595*, Hakluyt Society, 2d ser. no. 3 (London, 1899), p. x.

the administration of his estate was finally decided may eventually appear.

What was involved in preparing an expedition such as that of 1591? The manuscript does provide some new information on the business side, but a good deal of the reconstruction must be incomplete and conjectural. There were three parties in organizing and paying for an Elizabethan overseas expedition where plunder, discovery, and trade were all involved. First, there was the owner of the vessels taking part—there might be a number of owners or some of the vessels might be hired, but in 1591 there was, in effect, a single owner, with the *Daintie* the only "outside" vessel—and the owner might have a number of adventurers with him to spread costs. Second, there were the victualers who put up the supplies and equipment needed for the voyage. Third, there were the adventurers and seamen who went on the voyage. The first and second put a certain amount into the venture as investors, or merely paid their own way as adventurers in person; the last might get paid wages, as they did in this case, if the voyage was long and arduous. The normal practice was for total costs (including the capital value of the ships and their nonconsumable equipment) to be estimated after the conclusion of an expedition and set against total proceeds the value of ships and equipment brought safely back, plunder taken and goods acquired in trade. From the gross profits official charges—customs duty (5 percent on value) on goods imported and the Lord High Admiral's tenth (10 percent in goods)—had to be deducted. The residue was divided into three equal parts, between the adventurers, the victualers, and the men (the men taking shares according to rank, the others according to their investment). In 1591 wages as well as shares were paid to the seamen and these would be deducted from gross proceeds before division. Advances of pay were taken at Plymouth by men who then deserted the expedition. Before he sailed, Cavendish told Richard Hawkins he had lost £1,500 by these means[65] (though he may have exaggerated). In practice the sharp division was often obscured, some adventurers having underwritten the owners, some the victualers—or part of each—while a member of the crew might have invested as well as served for wages and shares.

The total cost of the expedition can be estimated only in a very rough way, but, using Dr. K. R. Andrews's careful estimates[66] and adding what we know of the ships and their equipment (which is not a great deal), we can get some idea of the sums involved:

	Ship, guns, munitions	Provisions (12 months)	Wages (1 year)
Galleon Leicester 400 tons	£3,500	£1,500	£1,200
Roebuck 240 tons	£1,750	£850	£1,000
Desire 120 tons	£600	£450	£550
Daintie (60 tons?)	£300	£300	£300
Black Pinnace (40 tons?)	£200	£200	£200

65. Hawkins, *Observations*, ed. Williamson, p. 20.
66. *Elizabethan Privateering*, pp. 32–50.

This would give us a total of £12,900, of which about £6,000 would represent the capital value of the ships and heavy guns. It is probable that the remainder is too low a figure in estimating for such a long voyage and that we should raise it to about £9,000 or £10,000, which would include a certain amount of money to meet contingencies and also provide some trade goods for disposal in the Far East, making the total £15,000 to £16,000. The capital investment in ships and guns was very largely Cavendish's own, together with the cost and fitting out of the *Daintie,* which was undertaken by Adrian Gilbert, John Davis, and their friends, and the guns he borrowed from Sir George Carey, so that this would account for about £5,000 of his investment. We have no precise total for the amount he was able to raise by sale and mortgage of lands he had recovered in 1588, but the figure was probably £5,000 at least.[67] The Gilbert-Davis syndicate was not only able to fit out the *Daintie* from the £1,100 they raised, but also to contribute to the victualing of the other ships. The detailed sums mentioned by Cavendish in the manuscript and in his will, some or most of which were investments, come to well under £1,000; there were numerous adventurers (investors) among the gentlemen and soldiers who went on the voyage and we might guess they put up money or materials to the value of another £2,000 or thereabouts. This would probably have been enough to launch the venture. It may be, indeed, that Cavendish had more laid aside from his gains of 1588 than sufficed to buy his ships and recover his lands and was able to put more into the expedition than we can estimate.

It is strange that he did not have, after his earlier success, the backing of any of the larger London merchants or syndicates which were speculating so heavily in privateering at the time. Several times in the manuscript he sneers at the businessmen who lent him small sums, and this may be the contempt of the amateur and gentlemanly adventurer for the crude profit-seeking of the City investor, but it may also reflect his failure to raise money in the City because his extravagance after 1588 had ruined his credit standing in the more cautious business circles that otherwise might have been willing to take a risk on the prospects of silks, spices, and bullion. Another contingency is that other, business-backed ventures were being planned and sent out by the Cape of Good Hope route at the same time as his and thus monopolized the capital which would otherwise have been at his disposal. He was poorly served, it would seem, by his victualers, and neither the *Galleon Leicester* nor the *Roebuck* stood up very well to the strains to which they were exposed. It may be that the quality of their equipment was below a reasonable standard also. The amateur was, indeed, liable to be cheated if he had not shrewd advisers to supervise his fitting out—and even sometimes if he had. But Richard Hawkins suggests[68] that Cavendish may have been a little credulous in accepting what his men told him was the true state of his ships, even quite late on in his voyage. Hawkins says he was wrongly persuaded to return from the Strait of Magellan to winter in Brazil, but once the men had got there they wanted to go back still further on the excuse that their equipment was too poor; soon they looked homeward, "one, with a little blustering wind taketh occasion to loose company; another complaineth that he wanteth victuals; another, that his ship is leake; another, that his mastes, sayles, or cordidge fayleth him. So the willing never want probable reasons to

67. Gwenyth Dyke, "Finances of a Sixteenth Century Navigator," pp. 108–16.
68. *Observations,* ed. Williamson, p. 88.

further their pretences." But it was Cavendish, with his individual mixture of sensitivity and toughness, who had to cope with these problems and to assess their implications. Rightly, or perhaps wrongly, they preyed on his mind. The thought both of failing in what had become for him a dedicated enterprise and of losing all that he had in hand and in England gradually overcame him and brought him to the depth of pessimism and despair which he showed in the manuscript. Looked at objectively the world was not lost for him. A young man of thirty-two who had inherited one fortune, made and largely lost another, could retrieve failure and a loss of property if his will remained resolute. This was the stuff of regrets and lamentations but not necessarily of tragedy. So, at the end, we are left with his pride and the phantoms of persecution which surrounded him as the companions of his last days.

Yet, just as Cavendish had written off the *Roebuck* and the *Galleon Leicester* in his pessimism toward the end, they had indeed survived and may have brought something of value with them. There had been valuables taken at Santos in the first raid and some of these may have survived on one or more of the three ships which came home. The *Daintie* was not heard of again, but it may be that with fuller records we should find that she too had returned and with a lading of value—indeed, there are some slight hints that this was so. The bright prospects he had seen for Davis had not been justified; the dark future he had seen for the rest had not been so black as his imagination had painted it.

Thus we come to an end. This account of Cavendish's last voyage is fuller than any that has been hitherto attempted, though it is still far from being definitive. Throughout it will have been evident how continuous our dependence has been on the manuscript which Cavendish wrote in his last days of life, that manuscript which has emerged, after a long obscurity, from the Bibliotheca Phillippica, and which helps so greatly to provide an authentic, living picture of the circumnavigator's last voyage and of his end.

Note on Transcription

The transcription has been done as literally as was possible without using special signs for abbreviation. Abbreviations have been spelled out; the added letters are in italics. There may be differences of opinion about the conventions used. Mostly, superior letters are retained in the expansion but brought down to the line: an exception is the "pre" contraction where the superior "r" has been ignored and the expansion made as "*pre*." Lacunae have been supplied in square brackets, largely from the text in Samuel Purchas, *Hakluytus posthumus or Purchas his pilgrimes,* 4 vols. (London, 1625) (abbreviated to Purchas, *Pilgrimes*), or from the extracts attached to the will, but occasionally by conjecture. The outer edge of the manuscript is frayed in some places and damaged in others, so that fragmentary letters, which do not always have the same appearance in the original as they do in photographs, have sometimes to be interpreted as well as possible, though one cannot always be certain. Occasionally Cavendish adds a flourish over a word which is not intended to indicate an expansion. These have been omitted but the small scrolls with which he completed a number of lines have been retained.

Cavendish does not capitalize consistently and is somewhat more sparing of capitals than most of his contemporaries. For "c" and "a" he uses forms normally employed for small and capital letters indiscriminately. For "m" he often adds only a very small extension of the initial flourish when he wishes to indicate a capital, and it is sometimes ambiguous. Both his "p" and his "v" tend to be intermediate between normal and capital forms. There is room for legitimate difference of opinion in regard to a number of these letters. Cavendish does, however, maintain a fair degree of consistency in capitalizing names of persons and places, using italic sparingly for a few of the latter, and he makes a practice of capitalizing the initial word of each page. He also tends to use capitals in words which have the implication of place names, as for example "the Island."

Cavendish's punctuation is not very consistent either. Many of his sentences are not clearly marked off by punctuation. He rarely uses a full point alone at the end of a sentence, though he does use the full point with a slant line "./" or "/" and this is exceptional in any other position. He uses the slant line alone more or less as a comma, but his favorite intermediate stop is a medial point, a full point above the line "·", which is used freely as a comma and sometimes also as a full point. It is by no means always easy to be certain whether he means it to be placed on or above the line. This use of a medial point was not unknown to his contemporaries but was not widely used. It may be found characteristically in Cavendish's inscriptions on The Hague map (see Appendix III), where place names are frequently followed by it. He uses commas but it is sometimes a little difficult to distinguish them from imperfectly written slant lines. His use of colons and semicolons is infrequent and it is not clear that here he was following any consistent convention in distinguishing between them. It is sometimes difficult to distinguish rests of his pen from punctuation.

The Last Voyage of Thomas Cavendish
1591-1592

T[homas] Cavendyshe
[his] [l]ast Voyage
written by [him in] 159[2]*

* The amendments in this line are highly conjectural.

1   Moste lovinge frinde, there is nothinge in this
     worlde that makes a truer triall of frindeshippe
     then at deathe to shew myndefullnes of love and
     frindshippe *which* nowe you shall make a *perf*ect
5   experience of, desiringe you to holde my loue
     as deare dyeinge poore, as if I had bynn moste
     infinitelye riche, the successe of this moste ∼
     vnfortunate Action· the bitter torment*es*
     thereof, lye so heavie vppon me as w*i*th muche
10   payne am I able to write these fewe lynes
     muche lesse to make discourse¹ vnto you of
     all the adu*er*se happes that hath befallen
     me in this viage, the leste whereof is my
     deathe· / but because you shall not be ignorant
15   of them I haue appoynted some of the moste
     sensibleste men that I lefte behinde me
     to make discourse vnto you of all these
     accident*es*: / I have made a simple will
     wherein I haue made you sole & onelie ∼
20   disposer of all suche little, w*hi*ch is lefte² /
     The Rooe Bucke³ lefte me in the moste ∼
     desoluteste Cayse that ever man was lefte
     in, what is become of hir I Can not Imagyn[e]
     but if she be returned into Englande⁴ hit
25   is a moste admirable matter / but if shee
     be at home, or anye other of my goodes ∼
     whatsoeu*er* returne into Englande I haue
     made you onelie possessor of them:⁵ /
     And nowe to Come to that villaigne
30   that hath bynn the death of mee and the
     decaie of the whole Accon, I meane
     Davys⁶ whose onely trecherie in

1. "discouerie." Purchas, *Pilgrimes* 4 (1625):
1192.
2. "as is left." Ibid.
3. *Roebuck,* vice-admiral of the squadron,
Captain John Cocke. Hakluyt, *Principal navigations* 3 (1600): 842; see p. 19 above.
4. She was back in Portsmouth by March 1593.
See pp. 35, 39 above.

5. "the same" deleted; "them," inserted.
6. The actual circumstances of John Davis's
voyage were very different from what Cavendish
imagined. With only a handful of men he reached
Ireland in June 1593 after incredible hardships.
Hakluyt, *Principal navigations* 3:842.

1

Moste lovinge frinde, there is nothinge in teys
worlde that makes a truer triall of frindeshyppe
then at deathe to shewe myndefullnes of lovhe and
frindeshyppe unto you, & all I shall make a profe
[I or] expoherence of, desiringe you to holde my lovhe
as deare & vemge poore, as as I I hae bynde moste
infmite to melhe, the shall yf I leys moste
unfortunate dertion, by & better tormente &
keprek, by I so beabie uppon me as sole, inmoe
payset am I able to write these selve lynes
inmoe leyst to make distones unto you, of
all the, as is happes that hate befallen
me in this viage, the leste we provys is my
beate, & but beraule you shall not be ignorant
of the sens I hate apoynted some of the moste
sufislege men that I leste behinde me
to make distonese with you shall leys
accdent & I I hae made a simple will
im greme I hae made you sole & onelie
shoste of all those lyttle which is leste
the more make leste me in the moste
desaluteste dange that ever man was leste
in, what is berome of her I dare not Imagin
but if she be returnede into Englande ett
is a moste admirable matter, but if she
be at me lome, or anye olher of my fleete
weather returne into Englande, I hae
made you onelie possesser of the
And noue to come to lesst trillage
teyt yay byme the deathe of me, and the
berause yf & A supole beason It maimes
sudenly, leys onely tre rebies in

1   Runinge from me hathe bynn An vtter ⁓
     Ruyn of all / if anye goode Returne by
     hym, as ever you loue me make suche
     frindes as hee of all others maye repe
5   leaste gayne·¹ / I assure my self yoᵂ wilbe
     carefull in all frindshippe of my laste
     Requestes· / My debtes which be oweinge be
     not muche,² there is 200ˡⁱ vppon a bande
     to Carewe Raleighe³ which he will infinitli
10   troble you for, you knowe his humor he
     onelie likes to bargayne satisfie hym in the
     same sorte, there is dewe to two merchauntes⁴
     in London vppon a byll of adventure ⁓
     which the Shippes are bound for 250ˡⁱ ⁓
15   which you maye sleightlie Compounde for· /
     For other adventures whatsoeuer the⁵ Run
     in the vittayles as all other adventures
     dothe· / I praie you doe this for me, Sir
     George Careye⁶ hath a byll of an 150ˡⁱ ⁓
20   venture which I gaue hym for fower Iron
     gunes, deliuer hym if the Roobucke be
     Returned 2 demye culveringes of brasse
     with myne Armes on them and his 4 Iron
     peices, they are to be knowe by his marke
25   which is a swanne·⁷ / Sir Henrie Palmer⁸
     adventured 20ˡⁱ, praie seen hym ⁓
     annswered / for private debtes I knowe
     of none, but hit may be my vntrustie
     servantes haue lefte some paltrie
30   sommes vnpaid, if you thincke they
     be myne I knowe you will vse your
     goode discretion in it· / There is
     a Bylle of adventure to Henrye ⁓

1. Preparations were made to interrogate
Davis on his arrival, though depositions have
not been found; he was exonerated and was able
to publish a public statement of his experiences
in *The seamans secrets* (London, 1595). See
above p. 41.

2. "not much &c." Purchas, *Pilgrimes* 4 (1625):
1192, who thereupon omits all matter down
to line 8 on fol. 2 following.

3. Sir Carew Ralegh (elder brother of Sir
Walter Ralegh) of Downton, Wiltshire,
b. *ca.* 1550 d. *ca.* 1625.

4. One of the merchants was Sir Thomas
Myddleton, a note of whose £50 advance was
entered in his journal. Chirk Castle MS F.12540,
National Library of Wales; see S. T. Bindoff,
J. Hurstfield and C. H. Williams, eds.,

Elizabethan Government and Society (London:
Athlone Press, 1961), pp. 256–63. The other
may or may not be the Elliote of Ratcliffe
mentioned on fol. 37 below.

5. "the," as often throughout the manuscript,
for "they."

6. Sir George Carey was knight marshal and
captain of the Isle of Wight, 1582–1603, and
from there assisted many legitimate and less
legitimate overseas ventures; he was a major
investor in Cavendish's enterprise and is
mentioned by him on fol. 38 below.

7. The swan formed part of the crest of the
Carey family and was used by Sir George as his
badge.

8. Sir Henry Palmer, naval commander, of
Tottington, near Aylesford, Kent, died 1611.

cuminge from me hathe byn in vtter &
ruyn of all, if I have good returne by
Gynd, as ever you tone me make sure the
winter as the of all other mayes rope
least gayne. // I assure my self you wilbe
carefull in all kinde shippe of my laste
requeste / my debtes will be owenge be
not suretye, there is 200li vppon a bande
to dardue releyges will she will must be
troble you for, you knowe his humor she
onelie likes to bargayne sati the gynd in the
same sorte, there is dewe to two merchant
in london vppon a bull of adventure
my shippe shippes are bounde for 250li
will you maye floiyetlie compounde for
for other adventures what soeven the som
in the vittayles as all other adventures
to the / I praie you doe this for me, the
George dakere hathe a bull is lau 150li
venture will I gave my for suer from
fund, cclui Gynn if the robucke be
returned 2 cemye duberinge of brasse
will myne dremes ore the and his 4 iron
poutes, they are to be done by the marke
let his a pronue. the Lewis palmer
adventured 20li & praie to be so
aunswered, for private debtes I knowe
of none, but he maye be my vintistic
servant have lefte some galthin
somes vnpaide, if you be sure they
be myde I knowe you will vse your
goode distretion in it — There is
the 23y li of adventure to Henry y —

1   Sakeforde[1] of ◇ - 300[li] ◇ - he is an hungrye man
    and one that will seeke muche, vse your discretion
    with hym. he Can Clayme nothinge but as a
    parte vitler,[2] if anye suche Importunate men
5   troble you Comforte theym with the Returne
    of the other Shippes, which trulie there
    is some hope of, if ever they Returne they
    Can not be but riche.[3] / but I moste vnfortuna[te]
    villaine,[4] was matched with the moste abiect
10 mynded & mutanus Companye that ever
    was Caried owt of Englande by anye man
    livinge / for I proteste vnto you that in ~
    goinnge to the Straightes of Magelanus
    after I was passed to the Southwarde of
15 the Ryver of Plate[5] and had bidden[6] the furi[e]
    of stormes · whiche in deede I thincke to be such
    as worser mighte not be indewred, I neve[r]
    made my Course to the straightes warde
    but I was in Continuall daunger, by my ~
20 Companye which never ceassed to practise and
    mutinie againste me, and haveinge gotten
    the appoynted place called Porte Desire[7] I
    mett with all my Companye which had bynn
    there neere 20 daies before me, and had n[ot]
25 my most trewe frindes bynn there, whom
    to name my harte bleedes I meane my ~
    Coussen Cocke,[8] I had bynn Constrained ethe[r]
    to haue suffered violence, or some other most
    disordered mishappe· / I Came into this
30 Harbor with my Boote, my Shippes ~
    Rideinge withowt at Sea, where I found
    the Roobucke[9] the Desire and the Pennis
    all which Complayned vnto me that the tyd[e]

1. Henry Seckford of Woodbridge, Suffolk (with his brothers Thomas and Humphrey), was engaged in both commercial and maritime enterprises, not all of them strictly within the law. He helped finance the venture, partly by accepting land under mortgage from Cavendish, partly by investing in victualing the ships. He was associated with Sir Thomas Myddleton in trading ventures, and as groom of the privy chamber and keeper of the privy purse had access to the Queen. He was knighted in 1603 and died in 1610. For his business activities see K. R. Andrews, *Elizabethan Privateering* (1964), pp. 26, 112–13, 121, 197, 244, 247–8.

2. Gorges is being warned to prevent Seckford from claiming any return on the voyage except for his investment in the victualing.

3. No clear indication of what returns there were from the voyage survives.

4. Purchas, *Pilgrimes* 4:1193, begins again, "But I (most vnfortunate villaine)."

5. The midpoint of the opening of the Rio de la Plata is at lat. 35° 02′ S long. 54° 53′ W.

6. "bidden" here and in Purchas, *Pilgrimes* 4:1193, with the meaning "challenged."

7. Now Deseado, lat. 47° 46′ S long. 65° 54′ W, located and named on the earlier voyage. The entrance is difficult, reefs fringing the northern side of the entrance (modern Punta Cavendish); the tide runs at 5 to 6 knots at the springs. Admiralty, Hydrographic Department, *South America Pilot,* part 1 (9th ed., 1945), p. 485.

2.

Cakeforde of, ƚ—300 ƚ, & he is an hungrye man and one that will seeke more, vse yor discretion wth him. &c than leavinge nothinge but as a parte bitter, if any thinge importunate men troble you don forte to him wth him he returne of the oleyns shipp, but I truelie thino he is from tonn of, if ever he retorne he can not be but very, but I moste importunate villaine, was matched wth the moste abiect minded mutanus companie that ever was caried out of Englande by anie man lininge, for I proteste vnto you that in goinge to the straightes of magelanus after I was passed to the southwarde of the ryver of plate and had bidden the furie of stormes wth indeed I lyked to be sure as worse might not be indevored, I never made my doubt to the straightes warde but I was in continuall daunger, by my companye wre never reassd to practise and mutinie againste me, and labouyge gotten the appointed place called porte desire & mett wth all my companye wch had bynn wth nere 20 daies before me, and had my moste trewe frindes bynn there, to put to name my earte bloude I meane my dompen doske, & had bynn constrained then to haue shedded violence, or some of the moste disordered mishappe, / I came into this harbor wth my 23 oate, my shipps w[]dowye wth put at sea, wch wre I fowe the robucke the deser and the shinn all wre complayned vnto me that the fir[]

8. "cusin Locke." Purchas, *Pilgrimes* 4:1193. The cousinship was through the Wentworths, Cavendish's mother's family. John Cocke (d. 1574) of Little Stanbridge Hall, Essex, married Elizabeth, daughter of Lord Wentworth, and their son and heir was the Captain John Cocke, who was with Cavendish. In 1587 (when he was described as of Prittlewell, Essex) he had applied for a grant of arms. See *Essex Archaeological Society Transactions* 3 (1865):192; *Miscellanea Genealogica et Heraldica,* 5th ser., 9 (London, 1935–37):322.

9. The *Daintie* was missing, though her captain, Randolph Cotton, had been on board the *Roebuck* when the ships were scattered. She presumably made for England after losing contact with the other vessels.

1   Ran so violentlie as they were not able to
    Ride but were driven a grounde, & · wished
    me in anye wise not to Come in with my
    Shippe for that if shee[1] shoulde Come
5   on grounde she woulde be vtterlie Cast
    awaye, which I knewe to be moste trewe· /
    And fyndeinge hit to be noe place for
    so greate a Shippe withowt her vtter
    Ruyne, I fourthewith Comannded them
10 to make them selffes redye to departe,
    they beinge freshe & infinitelie well ⁓
    Releved with seales & burdes[2] which in that
    place did abound· / My Companye being
    growen weke and feble with Continuall
15 watcheing pumpeing & baylinge, for
    I muste saie trulye vnto you there
    were never men that indured more[3]
    extremities of the seas then my poore
    Companye had[4] donne· / such was
20 the furie of the weste southe west and·
    southe weste wyndes[5] as wee were driven
    from the Shore 400 leagues and ⁓
    Constrained to beate from 50 degrees to
    the south warde into 40 to the north
25 warde againe before wee Coulde Recover
    neare the Shore,[6] in which tyme wee
    hadd A neewe Shifte of Seales[7]
    Cleane blowne awaye, and our ⁓
    Shippe in daunger to sinke in the sea
30 3 tymes, which with extremitie of mens
    labor wee recovered · in this weakenes
    wee departed for the Straightes being
    from that harbor 80 leagues[8]

1. "they" deleted; "shee" inserted.
2. The seals would have been mainly sea lions (southern fur seal, *Arctocephalus australis*) and the birds mainly penguin (Magellanic penguin, *Spheniscus magellanicus*), with a wide range of sea birds. Cf. Hakluyt, *Principall navigations* (1589), 643+3, 643+4; Hakluyt, *Principal navigations* 3 (1600):846, 849–50; Richard Hawkins, *Observations,* ed. J. A. Williamson (1933), pp. 74–79; Robert C. Murphy, *Oceanic Birds of South America,* 2 vols. (New York, 1936), 1:198–200, 427–52.
3. "greate" deleted; "more" inserted.

4. "dide" deleted before "had."
5. Cavendish was at this time in the belt of westerlies which dominates the forties.
6. He was being driven approximately eastward from long. 65° W to between long. 45° and 40° W, that is, from Patagonia almost to the Plate estuary.
7. "a new shift of sailes." Purchas, *Pilgrimes* 4 (1625):1193.
8. "eight leagues." Purchas, *Pilgrimes* 4:1193, though the manuscript is much more likely to be correct.

ran so violentlie as they were not able to
ride but were driven agrounde, & wished
me in anye wise not to come in with anye
shippe for that if they shoulde come
on grounde they woulde be vtterlie cast
awaye, which I judge to be moste trewe.
And finding hit to be noe place for
6 greater shippes wthout ther vtter
ruyne, I thervpon comannded them
to make them selues readye to departe,
the boouye of the & infinitelie woll
released with sealer & birddes wch in that
place did abounde. My company & being
growen weke and feble with continuall
watcheinge pompinge & baylinge, for
I muste saie trulye vnto you the
were never men at more extremities
extremities of the sea then my poore
companye did sustaine, sithe hear
the winde of the weste, southweste and
southeweste wyndes as wee were driven
from the shore 400 leagues and
constrained to beate from 50 degrees to
the southwardes into 40 to the north
wardes agayne before wee coulde recover
neare the shore, in wch time wee
& all the weste shifte of sealer
bleawin blowne alwaye of two our
shippe in daunger to strike in the ba
3 tymes, wth wch extremitie of more
labor wee recovered, in this weakenes
wee sayled for the stragglers beinge
from that harb harbor 70 leagues

1   And in ·18· daies wee gate[1] the Straightes in
     which tyme the men in my Shippe were growen
     extreamelie weake· the other Shippes Company
     were in good Cause by reason of there late ~
5   Releife·[2] and nowe wee had byne almoste 4 ~
     monethes betweene the Costes of Brasele & the straightes[3]
     beinge in distance not above 600: leagues which
     is Comonly rune in 20· or 30· daies·[4] / such was
     the adversenes of our fortunes, as in Cominge
10   thither wee spente the Sommer[5] & found in the
     Straightes the begininge of a moste extreeme
     wynter not durable for Christians· / In ~
     despight of all stormes and tempest so longe
     as we had ground to ankar in & tydes to ~
15   helpe vs wee beate into the Straightes
     some 50 leagues haveinge for the moste part
     the wyndes Contrarye· / at length being
     forced by the extremitie of stormes and the
     narrownes of the straighte,[6] being not able
20   to turne to windewarde noe longer, wee got
     into a harbor[7] where wee Ryde from the
     ·18· daye of Aprill till the 10 of Maye in
     all which tyme wee never had other then
     moste furiouse Contrarye wyndes, and after
25   that the moneth of Maye was Come in ~
     nothinge but such flightes of snowe[8] and ~
     extremitie of frostes, as in all the tyme
     of my life I neuer see none[9] to be Compared
     with them· / this extremitie Caused the
30   weake men in my Shippe onelie to decay
     for in 7 or 8 daies in this extremitie there
     dyed ·40· men and sickened[10] ·70· so that
     there was not 50 men that were able to
     stand vppon the[11] hatches·

1. "got." Purchas, *Pilgrimes* 4:1193.

2. According to Anthony Knivet (ibid., p. 1204) the *Roebuck* was in little better shape.

3. "and" deleted; "& the straightes" inserted in rather blurred ink.

4. On the circumnavigation his comparable sailing time had been 33 or 34 days. Hakluyt, *Principal navigations* 3 (1600):804–6.

5. Winter sets in sharply, under normal conditions, soon after the beginning of May.

6. "Straits." Purchas 4:1193.

7. This was what the men called Tobias Bay, with its "River of Pearles" which ran into it. Ibid., p. 1205. It would appear to be the modern

Pedro Sound, lat. 54° 04' S, long. 71° 35' W. Admiralty Chart no. 554.

8. In the Strait there is frequent snow from May to October and some throughout the year, while there is perpetual snow on land at 3,000 feet to the south and 4,000 feet to the north. *South America Pilot,* part 2 (1942), pp. 11–13.

9. "saw any." Purchas 4:1193.

10. Deaths and sickness are likely to have resulted mainly from scurvy, though Davis's men took the opportunity of gathering scurvy grass as an antiscorbutic at Deseado. See Hakluyt, *Principal navigations* 3:850.

11. "vppe the" deleted.

And in 18. daies wee gate the Straightes in
wth tyme the men in my Shippe were growen
extreamelie weake. the other Shipps company
were in good case by reason of theire late
releife. and nowe wee had byund almoste 4
monethes betweene the coste of Brasele and
bonige in distance not above 600: leagnes wth
is commonlye rund in 20. or 30. daies. / this was
the advertisemt of our fortunes, as in Domingo
thither wee shoute the Cold e pinud in the
Straightes the beginninge of a moste extreame
wynter not durable for Christians. / this
dispigete of all stormes and tempest so longe
as wee had grounnd to ankar in / that we to
helpe us wee beate into the Straightes
some 50 leagnes haboinge for the moste part
the wyndes contrarye. / at lengte boing
forced by the extremitie of stormes and the
narrownes of the Straughtes boinge not able
to turne to winddewarde noe longer, wee got
into a harber wgore wee rode from the
18. daye of Aprill till the 10 of maye in
all wth tyme wee never had other than
moste furiouselie contrarye wyndes, and after
that the monethe of maye was come in
no longe but sure sfligetes of snowe and
extremitie of foster, as in all the tyme
of my life I nevr se none to be compared
to the these. / theis extremitie causbe the
weake men in my Shippe onelie to deray
for m io 8 daies in theis extremetie here
dyod. 40 men and sikened 40. so but
there was not 50 men that were able to
stand upon the uppon the hatthes.

1   I fyndinge this miserable Calamitie to fale
    vppon me & founde that besides the decaye of
    my men & expence of my vittayle, the snowe
    & froste decayed our sayles and tackle,[1] and the
5   Contagiousnes of the place to be suche, for ∽
    extremitie of froste and snowe as there was
    noe longe stayeinge *with*owte the vtter Ruyne
    of vs all, what by theise extremities and by
    the daielie decaye of my men, I was ∽
10 Constrayned forthe*with* to determyne some
    Course, and not (for all this extremitie of ∽
    weather) to tarie there anye longer· / Vppon
    this I assembled my Companye together and
    shewed theym that my Intention was to goe
15 for China,[2] and that, that there was two
    wayes thither the on thorroughe the ∽
    Straighte · the other by the waye of
    Caba bona Spe·[3] whi*ch* Course I shewed theym[4]
    was as well knowne vnto me as the waye I
20 had vndertaken, and althoughe that fortune
    had denyed vs this passage yet I doubted
    not but soone to recover to this Cape where
    I shewed them I made noe doubte but wee
    shoulde releve our selffes, and p*er*forme to their[5]
25 Content*es* our intended viage. / theise
    p*er*swations *with* manye others w*hi*ch I vsed
    seemed to Contente theym for the present[6] /
    but they were noe sooner gon*n*e from me but
    fourthe*with* all manner of discontent*es*
30 were vnripped[7] amongste theym selffes &
    to goe that waye they plainlie and resolutlie
    det*er*mined neu*er* to giue their willinge Consent*es*
    some of the best and honestest sorte

---

1. The weaknesses of the *Desire* in these respects are stressed by John Jane, and of the *Roebuck* by Anthony Knivet. See Hakluyt, *Principal navigations* 3 (1600):843; Purchas, *Pilgrimes* 4 (1625):1205.

2. No specific objective had been named in his license (see pp. 19–20 above), but it was clearly known to all the men that China was their goal and that "China" also comprehended the Philippines, which Cavendish hoped to seize and use as a base.

3. "Caput bone spei." Purchas, *Pilgrimes* 4:1193. John Jane uses the form "Cape of Buena

Esperanza." Hakluyt, *Principal navigations* 3:844.

4. He means that he spread out a world chart and indicated on it his proposed course.

5. "our" deleted; "their" inserted.

6. John Jane says that John Davis at once pointed out to Cavendish that the fleet had no equipment adequate to make the long voyage. Hakluyt, *Principal navigations* 3:844. Knivet makes no mention of the Cape of Good Hope plan and says Cavendish "thought best to returne for the Coast of Brazile." Purchas, 4:1205.

7. "vnripped," laid open.

J ffyndinge this miserable calamitie to fall
uppon me, e ffounde that besides the decay of
my men e expense of my vittayle, the froude
e froste decayed our sayles and tackle, and the
ffurtagion shed of the place to be suche, for
extremitie of froste and snow as there was
noe longe stayenge wthoute the utter ruyne
of vs all, wcat by these extremities and by
the e daielie decaye of my men, J was
constrayned forthwth to determyne some
course, and not (for all their extremitie of
weather) to tarie there any longer, upon
this J assembled my company togeather and
shewed them that my intention was to goe
for Chyna, and that, that there was two
wayes thither the one thorough the
straightes. the other by the wayes of
Caba bona spe wch course J shewed them
was as well knowne unto me as the wayes J
had undertaken, and although that fortune
had denyed vs this passage yet J doubted
not but shone to recover to their daye wger
J shewed them J made noe doubt but wee
shoulde release our selffes, and perfume to ther
contente our intended viage. These
exhortations wch many of them vsed, J thes
seemed to contente thym for the present
but they were noe soner gone from me but
fourteen the all manner of discontent
were huryed amongst thym. theise
to goe that waye theye plainelie and resolutelie
determined not to give their willinge consent
some of the best and constest sorte.

1   Heareinge this theire Resolution, wished them
Rathere to put vppe a supplication to me then
thus priuatlie amonge theym selffes to muten
and murmer, which course mighte cause an
5   vtter Ruyn to fale vppon them all·[1] affirming
that they knewe me to be so reasonable, as I
woulde not refuse to heare theire peticon· /
Vppon this they framed a humble[2] supplicacion
vnto me, as they termed it / the effect
10   whereof was, that firste they protested to
spende their lyues moste willingelie for my
sake, and that theire love was suche to me
as theire Cheifeste Care was for me · and
they greved verie muche to see me put on
15   a Resolution which as they supposed woulde
be the end of my self, which was theire
greatest greef, & next theire owne lives
woulde Iminentlie[3] followe, bothe by reason
of the lengthe of the Course, all which they
20   muste performe withowt Relefe· / And ~
further wee had not lefte 4 monethes
vittaile which mighte verie well be spent
in Runinge A Course not half so longe: /
But if hit woulde please me to returne ~
25   againe for the Coste of Braseale where
they knowe[4] my force beinge togethere was
able to take any place theire· / wee mighte
both provide vittaile to returne againe and
furnishe our selffes of all othere such
30   wantes as these extremities had brought
vppon vs & at a seasonable tyme Returne
againe and so performe our firste Intention

1. Cavendish is trying throughout to demonstrate his determination to complete the voyage and to make clear that any variation from this course was imposed on him by the men. At the same time, his desertion of his sick men, and his violence in speech and action, may have made him appear to his men less reasonable than he asserted himself to be.

2. "an humbell." Purchas, *Pilgrimes* 4 (1625): 1193.

3. "immediately." Ibid.

4. "knew." Ibid.

Hearenige this there resolution, wished them
rather to put uppe a supplication to me, then
there privatelie amonge themp self so to mutter
and murmur, wch course myght rayse an
utter turn to spoile upppon them all. affirming
that they knewe me to be so reasonable, as I
woulde not refuse to heare there petitiones.
Apppon this they framed a humble supplicaco͠n
unto me, as they termed it / the effect
whereof was, that firste they protested to
spende there lyves moste willingelie for my
sake, and that there love was suche to me
as there chiefeste care was for me. and
they greved verie muche to see me put one
a resolution wch as they supposed woulde
be the end of my self, wch was there
greatest grefe, & next there owne liber-
wonte & mischiefe followinge, bothe by reason
of the lenghe of the course, all wch they
sum to performe wthout refuse / And
further wee had not leff 4 monethe
vittaile Owre myght to verie well be spent
in returninge a course not half so longe: /
But iff it woulde pleaso me to returne
againe for the coste of Brasale where
they knowe my force benige togethe we wase
able to take any place there / wee myghte
bothe provide vittaile to returne againe and
furnise owr self es of all other thinge
Owrte, as these extremities had brought
upppon us & at a seasonable tyme returne
againe and performe owr firste intention

1   Nowe I knowinge theire resolution and fyndeinge
    y^{t1} in some thing*es* theire reasons were not vaine
    begane more seriouslye to loke into all my ~
    want*es*· firste I founde my greateste decaye
5   to be in Ropes & sayles, wherein (by meanes
    of suche mightie extremities) I was vtterlie
    vnfurnished, for I loste a neewe shifte of
    Sayles² cominge thithere, and furder the
    Desier had bydden the like extremitie, w*hi*ch
10 I furnished so as I had lefte noe store at all
    for noe Shippes Carieth 3 neewe Shift*es*
    of Sayles / all w*hi*ch had bynn little Innought
    for me· / and laste of all our vittailes to be
    moste shorte· I was to fale into dewe ~
15 Consideration what to doe, I knewe well
    that the wyndes were suche and so ~
    Continuallie againste vs as by noe meanes
    hit was possible to passe thorrowe. for the
    violente snowes were such as in two ~
20 daies together we shoulde not be able
    to see 5 howers the place not a league over
    in breadeth,³ our Shippes not to be
    handeled in such extremitie of winde· noe
    nor Canvas to holde the furie of the ~
25 wynd, ou^r men so weake as of ◊ - 150 ◊ -
    men I had not in my Shippe in helth
    50·⁴ And this Shippe Cominge w*i*th
    all her Companye, was like 3 tymes to
    have bynn vppon the shore by Reason
30 of her vnyarye workeing·⁵ / These
    Causes made me vtterlie dispare of any
    passage at this Season / so I Resolved

1. That.

2. Suit of sails.

3. Such limited visibility, less than one and a
half miles for only five out of forty-eight hours
on account of snow, would not be unusual in this
area. See *South America Pilot,* part 2 (1942),
pp. 11, 13.

4. "fiftie in health." Purchas, *Pilgrimes* 4
(1625):1194. In normal circumstances fifty
men should have been entirely adequate to work

the ship, but Cavendish does not tell us how
many of those who remained able-bodied were
seamen.

5. "Vnyarie workings." Purchas 4:1194. The
word "unyary" is the negative form of "yare"
(active, nimble), and may be the earliest example
for a ship, as unhandy, not answering her rudder,
and, in the context, becoming unsteerable. I am
indebted to Lt. Commander G. P. B. Naish,
R.N.V.R., National Maritime Museum, Greenwich, for his comments.

6

Nowe & knowinge theire resolution and fyndinge
yt in some thinges theire reasons were not vaine
began more seriouslye to loke into all my
wantes. firste & founde my greateste decaye
to be in stoppes & saylers, (wherein by meanes
of surge mige the extremities) & was vtterlie
vnfurnisshed, for & loste a newe suite of
saylers cominge hither, and further the
deckes had byden the like extremitie, wch
& supposed so as & had lefte noe store at all
for not shipped barrels 3 newe suite
of saylers, all wch had bynd littell enough
for me, and laste of all our victaills to be
moste spoiled. & was to fall into deepe
consideration what to doe. & knewe well
that the wyndes were sure & so
continuallie againste vs as by noe meanes
yt was possible to passe thorowe, for the
violente shower were sure, as in two
dayes togehter we shulde not be able
to be & chowes, the place not a league
in breadeth, our shipper not to be
handeled in such extremities of winde, noe
nor daubes to holde the furie of the
wynd, one mon & meale at xv l x 50 ll
wch & had not in my shippe in Colles
so. And this shippe cominge w th
all her companye, was like 3 tymes to
have bynd vppon the shore by reason
of our buyarye watering. At this
panges made me vtterlie dispare of any
passage at this season, so & resolved

1   The Companye I woulde put owt of the haʳbor[1] &
       beate to get thorroughe so longe as the furies &
       westerlie wyndes woulde suffer vs·[2] but if ∿
       they Came vppon vs so as wee coulde not holde
5   hit vppe · wee woulde then beare vppe agayne
       & so accordinge vnto[3] theire requestes[4] goe for the Coste
       of Brasele · which they so muche seemed to desire,
       and I so much hated· / but in truth I was ∿
       forced to take that waye, for that there was
10   noe place where this Shyppe Coulde Come
       into to tarrye owt a wynter,[5] for *Porte Sa Iulian*
       is a barred harbor[6] over which two of my Shippes
       woulde not goe, and *Porte desire·* hathe[7] nether
       woode nor water and besides that the tyde
15   Runnethe so extremelye as hit is not possible
       for Anckors to holde, the grounde beinge so badd
       But the laste cause of all to be Considered was
       the sickenes of my men haveinge noe Clothes
       to defend them from the extreme Colde ∿
20   These causes & theire ardent desire to being owt
       of the Colde moved me to goe backe againe for
       that moste wicked Coste of Brasele where
       I incountered all manner[8] misfortunes which
       as I have vnripped[9] these former so I will ∿
25   breefelie declare the latter: Wee were beaten
       owt of the Straighte with a moste monsterous
       storme at weste southe weste[10] from which place
       wee Continued togethere till wee Came in the
       latitude of ·47·[11] in which place Davys in the
30   Desier / and my Pinnis loste me in the night[12]
       after which tyme I never hard of theme but
       as I synce vnderstode Davis his intention
       was ever to rune awaye·[13] this is godes will

1. The harbor was Tobias Bay (see p. 60 above), where he had put in on April 21, where he had harangued his men on going to the Cape of Good Hope, and which he had left on May 15. Hakluyt, *Principal navigations* 3 (1600):843; Purchas, *Pilgrimes* 4 (1625):1205.

2. The strong and gusty westerlies of the forties.

3. "vnto" inserted.

4. "according to their request." Purchas 4:1194.

5. He omits mentioning that he put in for two days at Port Famine (Sarmiento's former Ciudad Rey Felipe) to take stock of his resources. Purchas 4:1205.

6. Port San Julián, lat. 49° 11′ S, long. 67° 36′ W, the inlet being entered between Cabo Curioso and Punta Desengaño, four miles apart, the channel narrowing after two miles and opening into a basin which dries out at low tide; there are rocks and shoals in what is now a marked channel, with at least twenty feet of water at the entrance. *South America Pilot,* part 1 (1945), pp. 493–94; Admiralty Chart no. 1284.

7. "Port Desire had." Purchas 4:1194. In modern times, Deseado, though it has a bar, has at least twenty-seven feet of water at low tide. *South America Pilot,* part 1, pp. 484–87; Admiralty Chart no. 1284.

8. "manner of." Purchas 4:1194.

9. Revealed.

10. A storm at this season from WSW was not unusual.

11. Cavendish is unlikely to have been able to make an accurate latitude determination in such weather. The vessels had evidently made between 100 and 150 miles northing (though we do not

7

know his easting); he had probably only
recently passed Deseado.

12. To Davis in the *Desire* Cavendish appeared
to have changed course during the night as he
could not find him in the morning. Thinking he
might have put back to Deseado, Davis turned
back, arriving on May 20 and refitting there
until August 7. Hakluyt, *Principal navigations* 3
(1600):844–46.

13. Clearly Cavendish formed his view from
gossip on board after the event, but there is no
indication at all that it was well informed. In the
absence of adequate contingency plans for a
rendezvous, Davis could only take such action as
his judgment dictated. What he did was least
unlikely to lead to the reassembly of the fleet. The
failure in organization was Cavendish's, but
accident probably played a decisive part.

1   That I shoulde put hym in truste that should
     be thend of my lief, and the decaye of the
     whole Action· for had not these two smale
     Shippes parted from vs we coulde[1] not ⁓

5   haue miscaried on the Coste of Brasele for
     the onelie decaye of vs was that wee could
     not get into theire barred harbors, what ⁓
     became of theise smale Shippes I am not
     able to Iudge, but sure it is moste like they

10   went backe againe for *Porte Desire*·[2] a place of
     Releife for two so smale Shippes for they
     mighte lye on grounde there *wi*thowt ⁓
     daunger and beinge so fewe men they mighte
     Releve theym selffes *wi*th sayles[3] and birdes

15   and so take a goode tyme of yeare and passe
     the straightes·[4] the men in these smale shipes
     were all lustie & in health, wherefore the
     likelier to holde owt· / the shorte of all is this·
     Davis his onelie intent was vtterlie to

20   overthrowe me, w*hi*ch he hath well ⁓
     pe*r*formed·[5] / these shippes beinge parted
     from vs wee little suspectinge of anye ⁓
     trecherie· the Roobucke and my self held
     our Course for Brasele & kepte togethere

25   till wee Came to the latitude of 36.[6] where
     we encountered the moste grevous storme
     that ever anye Christians indured vppon
     the seas to live,[7] in · w*hi*ch storme wee loste
     Companye · we w*i*th moste extreme

30   labor and great daunger gotte the Coste
     of Brasele · where wee were ·15· daies and
     never harde of the Roobucke· wee Came to

1. "would." Purchas, *Pilgrimes* 4:1194.

2. "for Port Desier." Ibid.

3. "Seales." Ibid.

4. Cavendish's analysis of Davis's probable actions is a good one, though Davis went to Deseado as much from necessity as choice. Earlier Cavendish appeared to take the view that Davis deserted in order to make for home; here he assumes that Davis is bound for China, stealing a march on him with his two smaller and more mobile vessels.

5. The suggestion of deceit or treachery appears to have been nullified in the proceedings following Davis's return.

6. He would then be approximately in the latitude of the Plate estuary.

7. Gales in this latitude are less likely near the coast than farther east (in long. 55° or less). We have no information on his easting after he left the Strait. Winds in this season are variable between northeast through west to southwest. *South America Pilot,* part 1 (1945), pp. 37–38.

That I shoulde put by you in truste that shoulde
be the prude of my liefe, and the decaye of the
wholle ditision. for had not these two smale
Shippes parted from us we coulde not
haue miscaried on the coste of Brasell for
the onelie decaye of us was that wee coulde
not get into theire barred harbors, weat
became of theise smale Shippes I am not
able to iudge, but sure it is moste like they
went backe againe for porte desire a place of
releise for two so smale Shippes for they
might lye on grounde there wethout
daunger and beinge so fewe men they might
relese theym better noe saylers and burdor
and so take a goode tyme of yeare and passe
the straigtes the men in these smale Shippes
were all lustie & in health, wherefore they
likelier to holde out the ende of all is this
David is onelie intent was on otterlie to
ober the howe me with he & he ath so well
provided these Shippes beinge parted
from us wee little suspertinge of anye
trecherie the Robucke and my self held
our course for Brasell kept together
till wee came in the latitude of 36 wher
we encountered the moste grebous storme
that ever anye Christians indured uppon
the sea to livem with storme wee loste
companye. wee wth moste extreme
labor and greate daunger gotte the coste
of Brasell where wee were 15 daies and
never harde of the Robucke wee came to

2

1   An ankar in the baye of Sainte Vyncent·¹ and
     beinge at an ankar, there, the gent*lemen* desired
     me to give theym leave to goe a shore to some
     of the Portingales farme howses to get some
5   freshe vittaile² w*hi*ch I grᵃunted· willinge them
     to make a present returne, knowinge verie
     well the whole Countrye was not able to
     p*r*eiudice them if they willfully woulde not
     indaunger theym selffes· they went to a
10   sugar Myll harde by me³ where I rode for
     that was my speciall chardge that they ∼
     shoulde never goe a myle from the shippe
     where they gotte some vittaile and Came a
     borde againe verie well· the next daie in the
15   morninge betymes an Indian Came vnto me
     w*i*th Captain barkar·⁴ W*hi*ch Indian⁵ Ran
     from his m*aste*r at my laste being there· this
     savage knewe all the Cuntrey· he Came
     vnto me and said that beyond a poynte not
20   a Culveringe shote of, there was a verie
     Riche farme howse and desired 10 or 12 men
     to goe thithere· Captaine Barkar beinge on[e]
     whome I moste trusted in the Conduction
     of men & whoe ever was the moste Carefulles[t]⁶
25   in suche matters of s*er*vice · I appoynted
     hym to goe⁷ & to take some 20 or 30 men w*i*th
     him and willed hym as hee had anye ∼
     Respect or regarde of my Commanndement
     not to staye but to come presentlie awaie
30   fyndeinge anye thing or nothinge· / he
     fourthew*i*th toke 25⁸ of the moste principale
     men in the Shippe· and then yo*u*r Coussen
     Stafforde⁹ woulde by noe meanes be lefte

---

1. (The "2" at the top of this page indicates the number of the gathering.) The Baía de Santos lies between Ponta Mundaba (on Ilha de Santo Amaro) to the north and Ponta Haipú, its western shore being made up of the Ilha de São Vicente, the northern channel round which leads to Santos, and the southern, much smaller and narrower, to São Vicente. Cavendish's shore raids took place near the latter, in the vicinity of Ponta Itaipú.

2. "Victuals." Purchas, *Pilgrimes* 4:1194.

3. Knivet says they had anchored facing a sugar mill which stood on the shore. Ibid., p. 1205.

4. Captain Barker has not been firmly identified. He may have been the Andrew Barker of Bristol, the administration of whose estate was granted in 1593 (PRO, PCC Administrations, 1581–95,

PROB 6/5, fol. 67), but there were two members of the Barker family of Ipswich, Edmund and John, with Lancaster in 1594 (Sir William Foster, *The Voyages of Sir James Lancaster,* Hakluyt Society, 2d ser., no. 85 [London, 1940], passim), and it may have been John (Edmund being engaged elsewhere) who was with Cavendish.

5. The Indian, with another, had joined Cavendish voluntarily at São Vicente in January 1592. Purchas 4:1204.

6. "carefull." Ibid., p. 1194.

7. "appointed to goe." Ibid.

8. "fiue and twentie." Ibid.

9. For Edward Stafford's connection with Cavendish see p. 27 above.

an ankar in the baye of sainte vyncent. and
beinge at an ankar, there, the gent desired
me to gibe theym leave to goe a shore to sme
of the portingales farmes howses to get sme
freshe vittaile wch I grauntes. willinge them
to make present returne, knowinge howe
well the whole countrye was not able to
vindite them if they willfully wolde not
indaunger theymselffes. they went to a
sugar myll harde by me where I rode for
that was my speciall chardge that they
coulde never goe a myle from the Shyppe
where they gotte sme vittailes and came a
borde againe verie well. the next daie in the
morninge betymes an Indian came unto me
wth captaine barker. this Indian ran
from his me at my laste beinge there. this
savage endweade the duntity. he came
unto me and said that beyond a poynte not
a culberinge shote of, there was a verie
riche farme howsb and desired 10 or 12 men
to goe thither. captaine barker beinge on
whome I moste trusted in the condution
of men whoe ever was the moste carefull
in suche matters of service. I appoynted
him to goe to take sme 20 or 30 men wth
him and willed him whether had anye
respecte or regarde of my commaundement
not to staye but to come presentlie awaie
fyndinge anye thing or nothinge. he
hourtedlye toke 25 of the moste princepall
men in the Shyppe. and then ye constable
Stafforde woulde by noe meanes be lefte

1   Behynde they departed by 4 of the Clock in the ~
     morninge so as I did not see theire companye· /
     but what shoulde I write more than this vnto
     you, that they were all suche as nethere respected
5   me, nor anye thinge that I Comannded· / awaye ~
     they wente & by one of the Clocke they sent my
     Boote againe with Gynne wheate[1] and ·6· hennes
     and a smale hogge / I seeing noe returne againe
     of the Companye for they had sent awaye the
10   Boote onelie with men to Rowe her abord[2] I[3] was
     verie much[4] greeved, and presentlie returned the
     Boote againe, with message that I muche ~
     marueled they woulde tarie at a place so long
     with soe fewe men and further that hit was
15   not a hogge & ·6· hennes coulde releve vs, and
     seeing there was noe othere Relefe to be hadd
     I Chardged theym straightlie to Come aborde
     presentlie · thus havinge dispatched awaye
     my Boote for them I still expected their present
20   Coming aborde, all that nighte I hard ~
     nothinge of theym. the nexte morninge I
     shott ordinance yet I see[5] noe bote Come, then
     I wayed Ankor and made a borde into the
     Baye yet for all this I hard nothing of them
25   then I doubted with myself verie greatlie ~
     knowinge there was noe meanes lefte to
     make anye manifester signes to them to hasten
     awaye· all that daye I hard nothing of them
     in the Eveninge I set saile againe and Rane
30   into the shore so as I Rode within musket ~
     shotte of the shore,[6] all that night I hard
     noe neewes[7] of them· the next morning I sawe
     an Indian Came downe to the sea side and
     weued vnto the Shippe wee being desirous

---

1. Maize.

2. Knivet's story differs substantially from that of Cavendish. He says the party was sent ashore in his improvised boat made of "Sugar chests and barrell boords," but that when they sacked the sugar mill they captured "a great Barke" which they sent laden with food to the ships, and another lading of "Sugars and Guinee Wheate" the next day. The third day the "great Boat" did not return from the ship as the wind was offshore, so that when the shore party was attacked they had only the improvised small boat at their disposal, were unable to get away, and were overwhelmed. Purchas, *Pilgrimes* 4:1205–6.

3. "I" inserted.

4. "much" inserted.

5. "Saw." Purchas 4:1195.

6. "so as I Rode within musket shotte of the shore" omitted by Purchas.

7. "nothinge" deleted; "noe neewes" inserted.

Soe, vntill they departed by 4 of the Clock in the
morninge, so as I did not see theire companye,)
but what should I write more then this vnto
you, that they were all that, as well they reported
me, nor anye thinge that I comaunded. Alwaye
they wente by one of the Clocke they sent my
Boate againe with Kynne wingate and 6 others
and a small hogge, I seeinge noe retourne againe
of the Companye for they had sent awaye the
Boate onelie with men to rowe her aborde, was
verie greeved, and presentlie returned the
Boate againe, with message that I much
marueiled they woulde take at a place so lonely
with so fewe men, and further that this was
not a hogge, & 6 others could releve vs, and
seeinge there was noe other helpe to be had
I charged them strange this to come aborde
presentlie, this geavinge dispatched awaye
my Boate for them I still expected some, but
cominge aborde, all that nighte I heard
nothinge of them. the next morninge I
shott ordinaunce yet I see noe boate come, then
I weyed Anker and made a borde into the
Baye, yet for all this I heard nothing of them
then I doubled with my selfe verie greately
knowinge there was noe meanes lefte to
make anye manifester signes to them to hasten
awaye. all that daye I heard nothing of them
vntil the eveninge I sett sayles againe and came
into the shore so as I rode within a musket
shotte of the shore, all that night I heard
nothinge of them, the next morninge I sawe
an Indian came downe to the sea side and
wended vnto the Shippe was beinge desirous

1   To heare some newes caused a Rafte to be made
     for bote wee had none· & sent hit a shore and set
     the Indian aborde When wee see him wee
     founde hym to be our owne Indian w*hi*ch had
5   escaped awaye beinge sore hurte in 3 places
     hee toulde vs[1] that all they reste of our men
     were slayne w*i*th 300 Indians and 80 ～
     Portingales w*hi*ch in the Eveninge set vppon
     theym suddenlie·[2] / then I demannded why the
10   came not a borde· the Indian answered me
     that some were vnwilling to Come and the
     Reste did nothyng else[3] but eate hennes and hog*ge*s
     w*hi*ch theye hadd there in aboundance and y^t[4]
     they mynded nothing to Come aborde· / I leue
15   you to Iudge in what greef I was in to
     see 25 of my principale men thus baseli
     and willfullye Caste awaye, but I leve yo^w
     to enquire of others[5] the practises of these men lest
     in writenge vnto yo^w hit shoulde be thought
20   I did hit of malice, w*hi*ch I protest is farre
     from me · they beinge nowe deade and my
     self lokeinge Iminentlie to followe them· /
     Thus I was lefte destitute of my principale
     men and a boate· and had I not by greate ～
25   happe the daie a fore taken and oulde Boote[6]
     from the Portingales I had byn vtterlie vndon*ne*
     w*hi*ch bote I sent to an Ilande 15 leagues of
     to see if they coulde heare anye neewes of
     the reste of my Shippes she Returned w*it*hin
30   8 daies all w*hi*ch tyme I Remayned w*i*thowt
     a Boote, thus I was 16 daies before I hard
     neewes of anye of my Consort*es*[7] the 17th dai
     Came in the Robuck[8] haveing spent all her

---

1. "who told vs." Purchas, *Pilgrimes* 4:1195.

2. A Spanish account, published in Lisbon in 1602, referred to this battle, saying the Indians killed twenty-three men, including the son of a lord, while a surgeon, who proved to be a good Catholic, a gentleman (a "manceba cortesano"), another man, and an Indian (who had gone with the English) were taken prisoner. Martín del Barco Centenara, *Argentina y Conquista del Río de la Plata,* ed. Cárlos Navarro y Lamarca (Buenos Aires, 1912), fols. 224–26; see also Knivet, *Vária Fortuna* (1947), p. 33n.

3. "else" is inked over but probably by accident rather than for deletion.

4. That.

5. "others" inserted.

6. "an old Boat." Purchas 4:1196. But it was apparently this boat which had earlier been acquired by Stafford and his men and used for conveying supplies from the captured sugar mill, so that it could not have been captured by Cavendish the previous day.

7. "any" deleted before "neewes"; "my" inserted before "consort*es*."

8. The *Roebuck* appeared the very day they were to leave for Ilha de São Sebastião. Purchas 4:1206.

To theare some neewes caused a Rafte to be made
for bote wee had none. I sent hit a shore and set
the Indian aborde when wee sho the in wee
founde hym to be our dome Indian wch had
escaped away e beinge sore hurte in 3 plaics
hee tould vs that all they reste of our men
were slayne wth 300 Indians and 80
portingales wch in the eveninge set vppon
them suddenlie., then I demaunded why they
came not aborde. the Indian annswered me
that some were vnwillinge to come and the
reste did nothing els but eate themes and hogg
wch they had there in abowndance and y
they mynded nothing to come aborde. I leave
you to judge vn we at greos I was in to
sho 25 of my prinncipale men then bastli
and willfulli thuse away, but I leave yt
to eny iye of thes prattises of these men lost
in writeinge vnto yo els sevilde be thryst
I did thit of malice, wch I protest is farre
from me. they beinge nowe deade and my
sesf lokeinge imminentlie to follow them.
Thus I was lefte destitute of my prinncipale
men and a bogte. and had I not by greate
e, appe the daie afore taken and outte boote
from the portingales I hadd byn vtterlie vndone
wth bote I sent to an ilande 15 loagnes of
to see if they could spare any moduos of
the reste of my shippes the vetruall in
5 daies all wch tyme I remayned wthowt
a boote, then I was 16 daies before I herd
any neewes of any of my donsorte the 17 h dai
same in the Robart theboinis spent all theiy

1   Mastes but there misson · theire sailes blowne clene
     awaye & in the moste miserablest case[1] that
     euer Shippe was[2] in· all which mishappes ⁓
     faleinge vppon me and then missinge my
5   smale shippes wherein (vppon that Coste)
     Consisted all my strength haveinge noe ⁓
     Pinnises nor greate Bootes lefte to lande
     my men in, for they were all Caste awaye
     goinge to the straigth· / I not withstanding
10   (the wante of Bootes & pinnises) determined
     rather and not to be revenged of so base ⁓
     dogges, to venter the shippes to goe downe
     the Ryver a fore theire Towne and to haue
     beaten hit to the ground which fourthewith
15   I put in execution, and havinge gotten ⁓
     downe half the waye wee founde the River
     so narrowe by Reason of a shoulde, as all
     the Companye affirmed plainelie hit was
     bothe desperate & moste daungerus, for
20   the Ryver is all Ose·[3] and if a shippe
     Come a ground hit is[4] vnpossible ever to get
     of for there[5] Ryseth not a bove a fote of water
     & noe Ankors will holde to hals of[6] anye my
     Shippe in so narrowe a place, as wee
25   were almoste a ground in wendinge·[7] /
     Seeinge this apparente daunger I fourth
     with[8] bare vppe owt of the River where
     wee escaped noe smale daunger to get well
     owt for we had not[9] little more water then
30   wee drewe / and if shee had Come a grownd
     hit had bynn vnpossible ever to have gotten
     her of, by this meanes of not[10] passinge the River
     we were Constrained to let our Revenge
     passe[11] for our bootes were so badd & smale
35   as we durste put noe[12] men in

1. "cuase" altered to "case."
2. "were" deleted; "was" inserted.
3. Ooze, mud.
4. "is" inserted.
5. "there" inserted.
6. "hale of." Purchas, *Pilgrimes* 4:1195. The meaning is "will hold to haul off any of my ships."
7. Cavendish was apparently trying to pass into Santos Bay by the Rio de São Vicente, the relatively narrow and shallow westerly channel, rather than the main channel between Ilha de São Vicente and Ilha de Santo Amaro. See Gabriel Soares de Sousa, "Tratado descriptivo do Brazil em 1587," ed. F. A. de Varnhagen, *Revista do Instituto Histórico do Brazil* (Rio de Janeiro), 14 (1851):94–97; chart of São Vicente and Santos ca. 1570 in *The Troublesome Voyage of Captain Edward Fenton,* ed. E. G. R. Taylor, Hakluyt Society, 2d ser., no. 113 (Cambridge, 1959), p. 128; *South America Pilot,* part 1 (1945), p. 282; Admiralty Chart no. 1465.
8. "owt" deleted after "with."
9. "not" after "had" deleted; "but" inserted and deleted and "not" reinserted.
10. "not" inserted.
11. Cavendish sent a letter ashore to say he would return to revenge his defeat. M. del Barco Centenara, *Argentina y Conquista de la Río de la Plata,* fol. 225v.
12. "put" before "durste" deleted; "not" deleted after "durste"; "noe" inserted and "anye" deleted after "put."

master but there mission. theire sailes bloodinge thend
alwayes in the moste miserablest case that
euer shippes made in. all with my Cannon e
salvinge vppon me and then missinge my
smale shippes wherein (vppon that coste)
consisted all my strengh hatinge noo e
shipinge nor greate Bootes lefte to lande
my men in, for they were all Caste awaye
goinge to the straiytes / I notwithstandinge
(the wante of Bootes e pinnises) determined
rather and not to be revenged of so barbe e
doggse, to venter the shippes to goe downe
the Ryuer afore theire Towne and to haue
beaten hit to the grounde wherevppon by
I gaue in expedition, and hatinge gotten
Tonne lapse the daye wee found the Riuer
so narrowe by reason of a scoulde bar all
the Companye affirmed plainolie hit was
bothe desperate e moste Cannginge, for
the Ryuer is all ose, and if a shippe
come agrounde hit vnpossible ester to get
of for hyrselfe not above a ster of water
to noo tithors will ebbe to half of any me
shippe in so narrowe a place, as wee
were almoste agrounde in goinge e
cominge this apparaunte danger I durste
to le but bare here dut of the Riuer do sue
wee escaped not smale danger to get bothe
out for we had not litle more water then
wee drewe, and if she had come aground
hit had by me vnpossible ester to have gotten
her of, by this meanes of passinge the Riuer
we were constrained to let our Revenge
passe for our Bootes were so badd e smale
as wee durste not put any men in

1   Them· / Notwithstandinge wee landed & did them
    muche spoyle vppon theire farme howses & gotte
    some quantitie of freshe vittaile / this ∼
    place beinge not for vs consideringe our shyppe[s]
5   were not able to passe to theire Towne, and
    farthere our greate wantes did Constraine vs
    to seeke some Course of relefe which being not
    to be had there, bothe for that wee hadd ∼
    spoyled hit a little before, and also for that
10 wee coulde not Convenientlie Come to doe
    them anye preuidice, withowt moste loste to our
    selffes· / I determined to parte from thence ·
    & to goe to a smale Iland some 20 leagues of
    & there to haue¹ fitted all my necessaries and to haue
15 Caste of the Roobucke for that by noe meanes
    her wantes could by me be² furnished · and so
    at a seasonable tyme to haue gone for the
    Straightes of Maggalanus againe which
    entention, I muste Confesse I kepte moste ∼
20 secret for feare of some mutanye, but shewed³
    the whole Companye that I woulde goe for
    Saint Elena · where wee shoulde mete with
    the Carackes⁴ which Course I well knowe did not
    muche please them,⁵ for they desired nothing
25 more then returninge home into England
    & if I hadd but named the straightes they
    would fourthewith haue fallen into a most
    extreme mutanye for suche was⁶ the ∼
    miseries and tormentes they hadd indured· as
30 all the best sorte hadd taken an Othe
    vppon a⁷ Bible to dye rather then ever
    to yeld theire Consentes to goe backe that
    waye againe: / I knowing this · seemed

1. "haue" inserted in a somewhat shaky hand.
2. "be" deleted before "by" and inserted after "me."
3. "I" deleted before "shewed."
4. Cavendish had watered and rested the *Desire* at St. Helena in 1588, when he had not encountered, perhaps fortunately for himself, the carracks of the *Carreira da India,* which normally called there on their return voyage from Goa to Lisbon. He could reasonably regard it as his nearest and safest refitting base, with at least some slight prospect of a rich Portuguese prize in view.

5. The lack of enthusiasm was, no doubt, because the men believed that, if he repaired and, perhaps, revictualed the ships at St. Helena, Cavendish might well attempt to return to the Strait. A direct voyage to England would, in their current mood, suit them better.

6. "were." Purchas, *Pilgrimes* 4:1195.

7. "the" deleted; "a" inserted.

Item. Notwithstandinge wee landed & did then
vntill the spoyle stripped theire farme houses & gott
some quantitie of theire vittailes, theire
place beinge vpp so that considering our shipps
were not able to passe to theire towne, and
far theire our greate wante did constraine us
to steale some corne & cattle us beinge not
to be had theire, both for that wee had
spoyled yt a little before, and also for that
wee coulde not conveniently come to doe
them any spoile, I thoughte moste safe to our
vessels, I determined to parte from thence.

& to goe to a smale Iland some 20 leagues of
thence to fitted all my necessaries and to have
daste of the toobac for that by noe meanes
for wante coulde be by me furnished, and so
at a seasonable tyme to have gone thr the
straightes of Maggalanes againe with
entention, I muste confesse I kepte moste
secret for feare of some mutanye, but I shewed
the whole companye that I woulde goe for
Saint Elena where wee shoulde mete with
the caracks wth some well endued did not
much please them, for they desired nothing
more then returninge home into Englaund
& if I had but named the straightes they
woulde some have fallen into a moste
extreme mutanye for suche was the &
mischieffs and tormentes they had indured, as
all the best sorte had taken an othe
vppon the Bible to dye rather then obey
to yelde theire consente to goe that by that
waye againe: I knowing theire stomacks.

 1   To speake nothinge of that course, but ⁓
        Comforteinge theire despairinge mind*es*
        as well as I mighte · and theire greatest
        greef was for the wante of the smale
 5   Shippes w*i*thowt w*hi*ch they all affirmed
        (& that trulye) that wee were able to doe
        nothinge, for the portes where their towns
        stand were all barred harbors & that hit
        was not possible to get anye of these shippes
10   over them, whereby wee coulde Releve
        our selffes of such want*es* as wee were in· ⁓
        These thing*es* beinge alleaged· I seemed to
        passe over as slightlie¹ as mighte be
        but yet Comforted them that wee would
15   presentlie seeke some place of Releve
        w*i*th all speede / there was a Portingale
        aborde me whoe toke vppon hym to be a
        Pilote,² hee Cam vnto me, & telled me
        vppon his lief that hee would take vppon
20   hym to Carrie bothe my Shippes over
        the barre, at *Spiritus Sanctus*·³ a place
        indede of greate Releef & the onelie
        place in Brasele for vittaile & all other
        want*es* that we were [cu*m*e] in·⁴ / I knowinge verie
25   well that if I coulde bringe my shippes
        w*i*thin shotte of the Towne I should
        land my men · and farthere hit would not
        be in them to make resistance: the whole
        Companye desired this course ⁓
30   affirming that there was noe waye
        left to releue all our want*es* but this·

---

1. "most swiftlie" deleted; "slightlie" inserted.
2. The Portuguese had probably joined
Cavendish at Santos in December 1591.
3. Espírito Santo, now Vitória, Ilha de
Espírito Santo, lat. 20° 19′ S, long. 40° 16′ W.

4. "we" inserted; word between "were" and
"in" inserted, not easily legible, but it could
well be "cūe," abbreviated which expanded
would be "cume." Purchas, *Pilgrimes* 4:1196,
ignoring it, prints "that we were in."

13

To speake nothinge of that roome &, but
comfortinge theire despairinge minde
as well as I mighte: and theire greatest
greefe was for the wante of the smale
Shippes, without w[hi]ch they all affirmed
(& that truly) that wee were able to doe
nothinge, for the portes where theire tewnes
stande were all barred harbors & that it
was not possible to get anye of those Shippes
over them, whereby wee coulde releve
our selves of this wante: as wee were in
these thinges beinge allwayes & seemed to
passe over as [ ] as mighte be
but yet comforted them that wee would
presentlie seeke some place of releve
with all speede // There was a portingall
aborde mee w[hi]ch tooke uppon him to be a
pilote, hee came unto me, & tolled mee
uppon his liefe that hee would take uppon
him to carrie bothe my Shippes over
the barre, at Spiritus Sanctus a place
indede of greater releve & the onelie
place in Brasill for vittaile & all of[the]
wante that wee were in. I beleevinge heere
w[it]h that if I coulde bringe my Shippes
in this Coaste of the Towne I shoulde
lande my men. and therfore it would not
be in them to make resistaunce: the whole
Companye desyred this course
affirminge that there was no wayes
lefte to releve all our wante but this.

1   And that there they were in hope to fynde ⁓
      some shippes to repaire the Roobucke againe
      I fyndeinge there willingenes & Chardgeing
      the Portingale vppon his lief[1] to tell me
5   trulie whethere the Shippes mighte ⁓
      passe over the barre· *wi*thowt daunger, hee
      willed me to take his lief if ever the ⁓
      Shippes came in lesse water then 5 ⁓
      fathame *with* suche Constant affirmations
10 as hee desired not to live if hee shoulde not
      p*er*forme this· / I Considering the greatenes
      of our want*es* and knowing[2] righte well the place
      to be the onelie wished Towne on all the
      Coste to releve vs, fourthe*with* gave my
15 consent and thithere wee went[3] leavinge all
      othere ententions / wee Ankored before the
      Barre, & sent my bote to sound the barre &[4] found
      the depeste water to be but
      16 & 17 fote[5] the Portingale hym self going
      *wi*th them all over the Barre the moste
20 water to be but 3 fathame they Cominge
      a borde broughte me worde of the truthe
      I called for the Portingale & demaunded
      of him whye hee had so lied vnto me hee
      affirmed[6] that hee had never sounded the
25 Barre before & that he hadd brought
      in shippes of an 100 tunes & that hee mad[e]
      accompte there had not bynn lesse water
      then 5 fathame·[7] this mishappe was noe
      smale a maseinge[8] to me & all the Company
30 Considering our distresse for water and
      other necessaries & that the Rode was

1. The willingness of the Portuguese to put his life at risk had fatal consequences for him.
2. "knowing" inserted.
3. "went" deleted after "and"; "wee went" inserted.
4. "& sent my bote to sound the barre" inserted; "sent" deleted before "sound"; the ampersand before the caret was circled for deletion but has been restored before "sound."
5. According to a note to Knivet, *Vária Fortuna,* p. 35, "cinci braças d'agua" on the bar was precisely accurate. The modern chart shows a dredged channel through a bar which varies in depth from thirteen to eighteen feet. Admiralty Chart no. 546.
6. "who affirmed." Purchas, *Pilgrimes* 4:1196.
7. Knivet says, "the Generall thinking that the Portugall would haue betrayed vs, without any triall caused him to be hanged, the which was done in a trice." Ibid., p. 1206.
8. "amazement." Ibid., p. 1196.

And that there they were in hope to finde
but shipped to repaire the rudder againe
ff fyndeinge there willingnes & chardgeing
the portingale vppon his liffe to tell me
trulie whether the shippe might
passe over the barre wthout daunger, he
willed me to take his liffe if ever the
shippe came in lesse water then 5
fatheame wth suche & constant affirmationes
as hee desired not to liue if hee shoulde not
performe that. ff considering the greatenes
of our mouthe and knowinge the place
to be the onelie niefest downe on all the
coste to releve vs, hauing greedly gave my
consent and went whth their leaueinge at
other ententions wee Ankored before the
barre, & sent my boate to sounde the barre
16 & 17 of the portingale before going
wth them all over the barre the mosts
water to be but 3 fatheame hoy cominge
a borde brought me worde of the truthe
ff called for the portingale & emanuel
of him whether hee had lied vnto me hee
affirmed that hee had never sounded the
barre before & that hee hadde brought
in shippes often 100 times & that hee mad
accompte there had not byn lesse water
then 5 fatheame. This mishappe was no
smale a matteringe to me, all the companye
considering our distresse for water and
other necessaries & that the rudder war

1   So ill as[1] wee were scante able to Ride
     there, so as wee coulde nethere take in water
     nor doe noe othere busines, in this meane
     tyme while wee were scanninge of those ~
5   matters the Roobuckes Boote rowinge furder
     into the Baye see where three shippes were
     at an Ankor not farre from the Towne. And
     Came aborde and broughte me worde thereof
     at which neewes the Companye seemed much
10   to Reioyce, & all affirmed that they would
     goe with our Bootes & bringe them owt of
     the harbor / I shewed them howe muche
     the takinge of them imported vs and
     telled[2] them that althoughe the daie was
15   spent yet I thought the nighte not to be
     altogethere inconveniente if they[3]
     woulde put on mynde[4] to performe hit ~
     resolutelie / my reasons[5] were these
     firste they were not so sufficientlie ~
20   provided to defend them selffes at that
     instante as they woulde be in the ~
     morninge & further I tolde them that
     if they were not able to defend them they
     woulde take the principale & best thinges
25   owt of them beinge neare the shore &
     that if they hadd wherewith to defend ~
     them selffes hit woulde be lesse offensive
     to vs in the nighte then in the daie
     & wee in greatest securitie, and more
30   offensive to the enimye, especiallie this
     exploite being[6] to be donne one the water not ~
     landeing, these perswations seemed a little
     to move them for they all desired to stai

1. "that" deleted.
2. "told." Purchas, *Pilgrimes* 4:1196.
3. "for vs" deleted before "if they."
4. "on mindes." Purchas 4:1196.
5. "performe it. Resolutely my reasons." Ibid.
6. "being" inserted.

So ill as that wee were scante able to ride
there, but wee coulde neither take in water
nor goe noe oftner on shore, in this meane
tyme while wee were examininge of these
matters the roomingehs boote rowinge furder
into the Baye see where there shipps were
at an Ancor not farre from the towne. And
came aborde and broughte me worde thereof
at which newes the Company of sceamen wnt
to voiory, e all affirmed that they woulde
goe with our proctos e bringe them owt of
the harbor, I shewed them howe mutche
the takeinge of them imported As and
tolled them that allthoughe the daie was
spent yett I thought they mighte not to be
altogether inconvenient s but is they
woulde gent on mynde to o brinj et
resolutelie / my reasons were these
firste they were not so sufficientlie
provided to defend them selves so at that
instante as they woulde be in the
morninge Secondlye I tolde them that
is they were not able to defend them they
woulde take the principale e best thinges
owt of them bringe so neare the shore e
that is they fell in perillo to defend
them selves it woulde be lesse offenssive
to As in the nighte then in the daie
e moo in greatest securitie, and more
offenssive to the enimve, especiallie this
exploite beinge to be donne on water not
landeinge, those perswations seemed a litle
to move them for they all desired to staie

1   Till morninge yet some of them prepared
    them selffes; Cominge amongste them I ⁓
    founde them all or for the moste parte ⁓
    vtterlie vnwillinge to goe that nighte.[2]

5   Vppon w*hich* occasion I confesse I was much
    moved & gaue theme some bitter wordes &
    shewed them our case[3] was not to make ⁓
    detractions[4] but to take that[5] oportunitie
    w*hich*[6] was offered vs & not to feare a nighte

10 more then a daie & telled[7] theme plainelie
    that in refusinge of this I coulde staie ⁓
    there noe longer· for over the barre wee ⁓
    coulde not goe & the rode so danngerous
    as neu*er* shippes ridde in a wourse / and ⁓

15 further wee see all the Countrey to be fired
    rounde abowt[8] & that to lande wee ⁓
    coulde not w*ith*owt vtter spoyle to vs all·
    for our Bootes were naughte & further
    wee coulde by noe meanes be succored by our

20 Shippes· / so as I intended to departe the[9]
    next morninge from that place· / in the
    morninge there was almoste an vprore[10] ⁓
    amonge theme the moste of them swereing
    that if I woulde not giue them leave

25 they would take the Bootes & bring away
    those shippes of them selffes· / I Coming
    amongste[11] theme begane to Reprehend
    them for theire Rashenes & tolde them
    that nowe all oportunitie was paste

30 & that nowe they muste be Contented
    for goe they should not· they much ⁓
    importuned me & some of the Chefest
    of them[12] desired me w*ith* teares in their eies that
    they might goe, affirming that there

1. At the top of the page, "3" indicates the
gathering, and the faint "T" is a practice italic.
2. Knivet (Purchas, *Pilgrimes* 4:1207) stresses
Cavendish's unwillingness to let the malcontents
go at all, but says nothing, if they were to go,
of his preference for a night attack.
3. "cause" deleted; "case" inserted.
4. Apparently in the sense of "delays."
5. "suche" deleted; "that" inserted.

6. "as" deleted; "w*hich*" inserted in a somewhat
shaky hand.
7. "told." Purchas 4:1196.
8. "vs" after "abowt" deleted.
9. "nex" deleted at the end of the line.
10. "depart. The next morning, there was almost
an vproare." Purchas 4:1196.
11. "among." Ibid.
12. "of them" inserted.

till morninge yet some of them prepared
them selues; cominge amongst them I
founde them all or for the moste parte
Vtterlie vnwillinge to goe that nighte
Pppond wch occasion I rouseffe I warninge
moued I gaue them some bitter wordes I
shwed them our rase was not to make
extractions but to take that opportunitie
wce was offered vs I not to soiere a nighte
more then a daie I telled them plainelie
that in attendinge of this I wolde staie
there noe longer for ouer the barre was
wolde not goe I the rode so dangerous
as noe shippes ridde in a moneth I and
further wee se all the Countrey to be spied
rounde about vs I that to lande wee
wolde not do wthout some spoyle to vs all
for our Boats were many I vnfurther
wee wolde by noe meanes be shadoued by our
shippes. I bad I intended to departe the next
next morninge from that place. in the
morninge there was almoste an vprore
amongst them the moste of them pretendinge
that if I wolde not giue them leaue
the wolde take the Boats I bringe away
those shippes of them selues. I cominge
Amongest them beganne to reproue
them for their reasons I tolde them
that nowe all opportunitie was paste
I that nowe all they muste be contented
for goe they should not. they muche
importuned me I some of them desiret
vppon them
desired me not so leaue in this vice that
they mighte goe, affirming that they

1   Was noe dannger to be feared at all, for if they
    were not able to take them the woulde ∼
    Returne againe and that to departe *with*owt
    attempinge to doe this was a thing that
5   moste greatelie greved them, I knowing
    Righte well that if they landed not they
    coulde receave noe pr*ei*udice for if their
    shippes hadd bynn able to have *with*stoode[1]
    them it was in their power to goe[2]
10 from them beinge starke Calme, and ∼
    farder I knewe that noe shippes vseth[3]
    Brasele that be able to def*end* them self*es*[4]
    from a Cocke boote[5] muche lesse that they
    shoulde be of force to offend[6] theise botes
15 wherein there were so manye musketers
    as coulde sit on by one othere·[7] / I seeing
    there greate Importunitie was Contented
    to give theme leave to goe & this was
    my Chardge to Captaine Morgane[8] to ∼
20 whome at that pr*es*ent I lefte my directions
    that firste vppon paine of his lief hee
    shoulde not lande at all what oportuniti
    so ever there was offered & that if hee
    see anye dannger in Cominge to these
25 Shippes that hee should attempt noe
    furthere but returne aborde agayne· /
    but Contraryewise if hee see that the
    place was suche as wee might land *with*owt
    two much disadvantage, & if that[9] wee might
30 land on plaine ground free from wood*es*
    or Busshes hard a fore[10] the towne that

1. "to withstood." Purchas, *Pilgrimes* 4:1196.

2. "haue gonne" deleted; "goe" inserted.

3. "vse." Purchas, *Pilgrimes* 4:1196.

4. While some of the sugarmen trading from
Brazil were large and sometimes reasonably
well armed, there were few vessels in Brazil
engaged in protective duties or fit to engage
marauding foreigners. An occasional Spanish war
vessel was sent to patrol the coast when English
and French traders and raiders were active.

5. The cock-boat was the smaller of the two
ship's boats when she carried more than one.
The implication here is ironical.

6. "defend" deleted; "offend" inserted.

7. Confirmed by Knivet. Purchas 4:1206.

8. It has not proved possible to identify the
Captain Morgan mentioned here.

9. "that" inserted.

10. "before." Purchas 4:1196.

was noe dannger to be feared at all, for if they
were not able to take them the wou[l]de
returne againe and that to departe without
attemptinge to doe this was a thinge that
moste greatelie greved them, I knowinge
right well that if they landed not they
woulde retreate noe whidre for if they
were hald by me able to saue our goode
them it was in their power too from
them beinge starke calme, and
farder I knewe that noe shippes able
brasele that be able to defend themselfe
from a borte boote much lesse that they
woulde be of force to defend them selfes
wherein there were so many inspectors
as woulde set on by one of them. I beinge
there greate importunitie was contented
to give them leave to goe, this was
my charge to captaine Morgane to
whome at that instant I left my direction
that firste uppon paine of his liefe he
woulde not lande at all in that oportunitie
so over there was offered that if he
se any dannger in cominge to those
shippes that you should attempt noe
furthere but returne aborde againe.
but contrary doubles if you se that the
place was such as wee mighte hand wombe
two much disadvantag, or if wee might that
land on plaine grounde free from woode
or bushes sand a fire the towne that

1   Then he would p*re*sentlie repaire vnto me
    againe & I and so manye as these badd botes
    woulde Carie, woulde p*re*sentlie land vppon
    them, thus my bootes departed f*ro*m me ⁓
5   haveinge some 80¹ men as well furnished
    w*i*th weapons as hit is possible to sorte ⁓
    suche an number w*i*thall, nowe yo^w shall
    vnderstande that in the nighte the
    Portingales hadd haled² theire shippes hard
10 a fore the Towne,³ the River where⁴
    the Towne stoode on was not a bove a burde
    Bolte shotte⁵ over & halfe a myle from the towne where
    the Shippes Rode the nighte wee Came
    in, they had neewe Caste vppe two ⁓
15 smale trenches on eache side the River
    one where they hadd planted some
    2 small bases·⁶ a peece vppon a hill: right
    over them was⁷ thicke woodes & greate
    Rockes so that if anye were possessed of
20 them they mighte but tumble stones downe
    & beate awaye a 1000⁸ men, the trench
    on the wester side of the River shoote
    at our Bootes once or twise: vppon that
    the began to bethincke⁹ w*i*th them self*f*es
25 what to doe, captayne¹⁰ Morgan affirmenge
    the place to be verie narrowe & that
    they Coulde not well passe hit w*i*thowt
    dannger Consideringe the manye men in
    theire Bootes & also the Chardge w*hi*ch I
30 hadd given was such, as if they see
    anye¹¹ daunger they should p*re*sentlie ⁓
    Repaire aborde & certifie me & not to ⁓

1. The "0" in "80" has been stroked through as to read "8," but "80" must stand. Knivet (Purchas, *Pilgrimes* 4:1206) gives 120 (incidentally stating that Morgan's second in command was Lieutenant Royden, whom Cavendish does not mention), while M. del Centenara (*Argentina y la Conquista del Río de la Plata*, fols. 226–27), claims that in the end some 110 were killed.

2. "hailed." Purchas 4:1197.

3. Espírito Santo, later Vitória, on the Baía de Espírito Santo.

4. Altered from "whereon."

5. Bird-bolt-shot was the distance a light arrow, or crossbow quarrel used for shooting birds, would travel. It was a comparatively short distance.

6. Small cannon, English specimens having a bore of 1.25 inches and firing a half-pound shot.

7. "were." Purchas 4:1197.

8. "away 1000." Ibid.

9. "to thinke." Ibid.

10. "Capt." deleted; "captayne" inserted.

11. "such if they saw any." Purchas 4:1197.

Then he woulde p[re]sentlie repaire vnto me
againe, & I and so manye as those badd that
woulde tarie, woulde p[re]sent[e] land vppon
them, thus my bootes departed from me
& aberinge some 8th men as well furnished
w[i]th weapons as that is possible to sett[e]
suche an number w[i]thall, nowe y[ou] shall
vnderstande that in this mighte the
portingales had haled there shipp[e]s yet
afore the Towne, the River wheron
the Towne stoode on was not a bowe a shute
broade [from the Towne]
bolte shotte ouer, half a myle, where
the Shipper rode this mighte was came
in, they had neede take hyde twoe
smale trenches on eather side thereuppon
onely w[h]ere they had planted some
2 smale bases a p[ar]te vppon a fillinge sh-
oer theare was thirtie woodes & greate
forked so that if anye were possessed of
them they mighte but tumble stones downe
& beate away a 1000 men, the trenches
on the wester side of the River stoode
at our bootes cominge or twise, suppose that
he began to bethincke w[i]th hym selfe
what to doe, Captayne morgan affirminge
the place to be verie narrowe that
they woulde not well passe it w[i]thowt
daunger donsheringe the manye men i[n]
theire bootes & also the charge w[hi]ch I
hadd given was such, as if they had
anye daunger they shoulde but leave
repaire aboell[e] sertifie me[e] not to

1   Passe anye farder[1] till they had vnderstoode
     my farder determination· this *Master* Morgane
     made knowne amongste them, vppon
     this · some of hare braine sailers[2] begane
5   to sweare that they never thoughte other
     then that hee was a Cowarde & nowe hee
     well shewed hit[3] that durste not land ⁓
     vppon a bable diche as they tearmed hit·[4] /
     vppon this the gentleman[5] was verie muche moved
10   & annswered them that they should fynd
     hym to be none suche as they accompted
     him· & that Come what could happen
     him he woulde lande: vppon this in[6]
     they put the Bootes betweene the two ⁓
15   sconces that on the easter[7] thei[8] had not seene
     & the Bootes beinge hard vppon hit were
     shote at and in the beggest Boote they
     hurte two & killed one with that shote /
     vppon this they determined that the
20   smale Boote with theire Companye
     should lande on the wester syde & the
     other to lande on the easter side · the ⁓
     smale Bote landed firste & that plac
     haueinge but fewe in hit · they being not
25   able to defend them selffes Rane away
     so that our men entred peaceable withowt
     hurte of anye· the other bote drawinge
     muche water was a ground before shee[9]
     Came neere the Shore so as they that
30   landed were fayne to wade above
     knee highe in water· nowe the place

1. "further." Purchas, *Pilgrimes* 4:1197.

2. "some of the hairbraine sailers." Ibid.

3. "will shew it." Ibid.

4. A bauble ditch, in the contemporary scornful language, was equivalent to a toy ditch, one of no value for defense.

5. "gent" deleted; "gentleman" inserted.

6. "they" at the end of the line deleted and inserted at the beginning of the next.

7. "easter side." Purchas 4:1197.

8. "thei" inserted.

9. "they" deleted; "shee" inserted; "before they." Purchas 4:1197.

passe any farder till they had vnderstoode
any farder determination that mr Morgane
made knowne amongst them, vppon
this some of there browne sailers begane
to sweare that they never knew other
then that hee was a Edwardes, none hee
meett esteem[ed] it that durste not land
vppon a cable in case they fearmed it
                                gentleman
vppon this the gent was borne him so much
Cannswered them that they shoulde and
ynt to be none snsse as they attempted
him that come what it could happen
him he woulde lande, vppon this in the
they put the Boote betweene the two
romes that on the easter had not bene
& the Boote borne & Card vppon this were
sete at and in the byggest Boote they
hyrte two & killed one & so that past
vppon this they determined that the
smalest Boote wth theire company
puld lande on the wester syde & the
other to land on the easter syde. the
smale Bote landed first & that place
sauoringe but those in it. they beinge not
so that our men ordred peaceable to Litel
botte of same. the other bote drewinge
muche water was a grounde before they
coulde neere the shore, so as they that
landed were fayne to wade above
knee hyghe in water, & soe the place

1 Or sconce was in highe som*me* 10 fote made of
   stone (Captaine Morgan more resolute then ∼
   discreeteli[1]) scaled the wale and 10 more w*i*th
   him, w*hi*ch wente owt of the bote together, then
5 the Indians[2] & Portingales shewed them sel*ff*es
   and· w*i*th greate stones from over the trenche ∼
   killed Morgan & 5 more & the reste of them ∼
   beinge sore hurte retired to the bote, w*hi*ch by
   this tyme was so filled w*i*th Indian arrowes
10 as of 45 men beinge in the boote there escaped
   not 8 of them vnhurte some havinge 3 arrowes
   stickeinge in them some 2· and there was none
   w*hi*ch escaped w*i*th one wounde,[3] the furie of those
   arrowes cominge so thicke & so manye of them
15 beinge spoyled the put the Boote from the shore
   leaveinge the reste on lande a spoyle for the ∼
   Indians, by this tyme there Came 2. bootes full of
   lustie Portingales & some spaniardes[4] they
   knowinge the sconce on the wester side to be
20 weaklie manned, came w*i*th theire bootes to
   the fortes side where my men[5] had entred
   not knowinge as hit should seeme that
   our men had taken hit, they let them Come
   w*i*th theire bootes harde to the fortes side· one
25 of them Rune[6] a shore w*hi*ch was fullest of men
   then our men let flye theire musketes at them
   & spoyled & killed all[7] that were in ∼
   that Boote, the other seinge theire fellowes
   speeded[8] so ill Rowed backe againe w*i*th all their
30 force & gotte the Towne againe: in this
   meane tyme the greate boote beinge gotten
   of· the Called to them in the sconce and ∼
   willed them to forsake the forte and to

1. "more resolutely then discreetely." Purchas,
Pilgrimes 4:1197.

2. The people of this region were apparently
members of the Tupinaquin tribe of the Tupi-
Guarani Indians. Alfred Metraux, *La
Civilisation matérielle des tribus Tupi-Guarani*
(Paris, 1928), p. 14.

3. "escaped without wound." Purchas 4:1197.

4. Spanish reinforcements may have been called
for and have arrived, or else these may have simply

been Spaniards who were resident in Espírito
Santo. There is no mention of Spaniards being
present in M. del Barco Centenara, *Argentina y
Conquista del Río de la Plata,* fols. 226v–27.

5. From "where my men" to "the fortes side" in
line 24 omitted by Purchas 4:1197.

6. "ran." Ibid.

7. "the men" deleted after "all."

8. "speed." Purchas 4:1197.

or froute was ni highe stone 10 fote made of
stope, Captaine Morgyn more resolute then he
fristtetheld staled the whale and 10 more with
him, wt wente out of the bote togethver, then
the Indians & portingales shved themselffe
and inly greate tones from over the trence &
killed morgan & more & the reste of them
beinge sore hurte retired to the bote, yet by
his tyme was so filled wt Indian arrowes
as of 45 men beinge in the bote there escaped
not 8 of them vnhurte some havinge 3 arrowes
strikeinge in them somes 2, and there was none
wt escaped wt oute wounde, the furie of these
arrowes cominge so thicke & husavy of them
beinge spoyled the put the bote from the shore
leaveinge the reste on lande a spoyse for the
Indians, by this tyme there came 2 botes of
lustie portingalles & some Spanniardes thy
knowinge the stonte on the wester syde to be
weakelie manned, came wt her there botes to
the porter syde were my men & ad entred
just knowinge as yet reputed seme that
onr men had taken hitt, thy let there come
inly there botes harde to the porter syde one
of them tyme a shore wt was fullest of men,
shen onr men lot flye there muskotes at them
& spoyled & killed all the men that were in
that Bote, the other beinge there soldres
seekd so ill toward barke againe wt all theire
force & gotte the Towne againe in the
meane tyme the greate bote beinge gotten
of, thy called to them in the shore and
to lead them to spoyse the forte and to

1   Come & helpe them for they toulde them that all
     their men were spoyled and slaine, vppon this
     the straighte Came owt of the sconce againe
     and retired to theire boote, they rushinge[1] in
5   altogethere into the boote shee Came one ground
     so that of they coulde not gett hir / but some
     muste goe owt of her againe 10 of the ⁓
     lustiest men went owt[2] againe & by that
     tyme the Indians were Come downe into the
10   forte againe & shotte at our men, they w*hi*ch
     were a lande p*er*ceaveinge the arrowes flye
     amonge them rane againe at the forte syde[3]
     & shotte in at the loope hole[4] w*i*th their ⁓
     musketes / by this the bote was gotte of, and
15   one, that was M*aster* of the Roobucke[5] a moste
     Cowardlie villaigne that euer was borne
     of a woman he Caused them in the bote to Ro[we]
     awaye & so lefte those braue, men a spoyle
     for the Portingales yet the waded vppe to the
20   neckes in the water to them & yet these
     merciles villaignes in the Boote would[6] haue
     noe pittie on them · theire excuse was ⁓
     that the Bote was so full of water that
     had they Come in shee woulde haue suncke
25   w*i*th all them in her / thus vielye were
     these poore men loste[7] · and by this tyme
     they[8] w*hi*ch were landed on the other side·
     the greate bote not beinge able[9] to Rowe ner[e]
     the shore to releue them, were killed w*i*th
30   stones by the Indians, beinge thus ⁓

1. "who rushing." Purchas, *Pilgrimes* 4:1197.
2. "went out, and." Ibid.
3. "to the forts side." Ibid.
4. "lower hold." Ibid.
5. Possibly Robert Tharlton. See p. 106 below.
6. "will" deleted; "would" inserted in a somewhat shaky hand.
7. "lost. By this time." Purchas 4:1197.
8. "those." Ibid.
9. "not" inserted before "beinge"; "note" deleted before "able."

done & tould them for he y tould them that all
their men were spoyled and slayne, vppon this
they straight came out of the towre againe
and retired to theire boote, they vnfemige in
altogether into the boote they came dne from
so that of they could not yett hir, but some
must goe out of her againe 10 of the
lustiest men went out againe, & by that
tyme the Indians were come downe into the
forte againe, & shotte at our men, they not
were a lande portabemge the arrowes flye
amonge them rane againe at the forte who
& shotte in at the loope hole in the pir,
mufketes by feir the boote awas yotte of, and
one, the pt was one of the roobrule a most
dowardelie villayne that euer was borne
of a woman & caufed the end in the boote to be
away & so lefte the ps braue men a spoyle
for the portingales, yet they waded vppe to the
nockes in the water to them & yet the most
merciles villaynes in the boote would haue
noo pittie on them the fire cxcufe was
that the Boote was so full of water that
had they done in she should haue finke
or shall them in she, ther victyls were
to be poore men lofte. and by this tyme
they were now landed on the other fide.
the greate boote bemge not able to come nere
the shore to releue hem, were killed whilst
stoned by the Indians, bemge thus

1   Willfullie & vndiscreetelie spoyled, which you
    maye well *per*ceave if you loke into theire ~
    landeinge especiallie in suche a place as they
    coulde not escape killinge w*i*th stones· they ~
5   Returned a borde againe, haveinge loste 25[1]
    men whereof 10 of them were lefte a shore
    in suche sorte as I haue showed you· / When
    the bootes Came to the shippes side, there were
    not 8 men in the biggest boote w*hi*ch were not
10 moste grevouslie wounded.[2] I demanndeing[3]
    of them the cause of all theire mishappes[4]
    & howe they durste lande Consideringe my
    straighte Comanndement to the Contrarie /
    they annswered me that there was noe fault
15 in Captaine Morgane, but the greatest ~
    occasion of all this spoyle vnto them[5] happened
    vppon a Controu*er*sie betweene the Captaine
    and those souldiers that landed w*i*th him, &
    were killed at the forte, for theire ill speaches &
20 vrgeinge of Captaine Morgane was the cause
    that he landed Contrarie to my Comanndem*en*t
    & vppon suche a place as they all Confessed
    40 men were sufficient to spoyle 500. I lev[e]
    hit to yo*u*rself to Iudge of what a sighte hit
25 was to mee to see so manye of my beste men
    thus willfullie spoyled havinge not lefte
    in my Shippe 50 sounde men· so as we we[re]
    noe more than able to waye our Ankors w*hi*ch
    wee the next morninge did·[6] & fyndeinge hi[t]
30 Calme we were Constrained to Come to an anco[r]

1. "fiue and twenty." Purchas, *Pilgrimes* 4:1197.

2. Knivet (ibid., p. 1206) gives 80 and 40 surviving, almost all of the latter with at least one wound. M. del Barco Centenara (*Argentina y Conquista del Río de la Plata,* fols. 226v–27) says 110 were killed, while John Vincent (alias Yates) said 8 men, including an Irishman and a man named Robert Arundell, were taken prisoner (PRO, S.P.12/245,33).

3. "demanded." Purchas 4:1197.

4. "cause of their mishappes." Ibid.

5. "to them." Ibid.

6. "which (the next morning) wee did." Ibid., p. 1198.

w willefullie vndiskretelie spoyled, wch y^u
maye well greave if you loke into theire
landinge especiallie in suche a place as they
coulde not escape killinge wth stones. they
Returned aborde againe, havinge lost 25
men wherof 10 of them were lefte ashore
in suche sorte as I have shewed you. when
the bootes came to the shippes side, there were
not 8 men in the biggest boote wch were not
moste grevouslie wounded. I demaundinge
of them the cause of all theire mishappes
& who they durste lande consideringe my
straighte commaundement to the contrarie,
they answered me that there was no skull
in Captaine morgane, but the greatest
occasion of all this spoyle vnto us happened
vppon a controversie betweene the Captaine
and those souldiers that landed wth him, &
were killed at the forte, for theire ill speeches &
persuadinge of Captaine Morgane was the cause
that he landed contrarie to my commaundm^t
vppon suche a place as they all confesse
40 men were sufficient to spoyle & do. I leave
it to yor selfe to Judge of what a sighte it
was to me to see so manye of us so faste men
thus willfullie spoyled havinge no^t lefte
in my shippe so shuide men. so as we are
now more then able to waye our Anchors w^{ch}
we the next morninge did. & findinge the
calme we were constrained to come to an anco

1   Againe for my onelie intention was to gett
    owt of that badd Rode¹ & to put of into the
    sea & there to determye what to doe, for
    that place was not for vs to tarie in for the
5   Rode was so badde as wee were not able to ⁓
    helpe our selues with a bootes ladeinge of freshe
    water whereof wee stoode in noe smale ⁓
    wante of: in this daies staye in the Roode I
    comforted these distressed poore men what
10 I mighte, and I founde moste of theire ⁓
    desires to returne againe into Englande /
    I let them vnderstande howe² wee ⁓
    woulde go³ backe againe to the Ilande of Saynt
    Sabastion,⁴ and there wee woulde water &
15 doe our other necessarie busines·⁵ and there
    to make⁶ a resolute determinacion of the
    reste of our proseedinges · this course
    seemed to like them all verie well, but the
    Companye in the Roobuck instantelie ⁓
20 desired nothinge more then to returne
    home, all affirminge that hit was pittie
    such a shippe shoulde be caste of, but
    in truthe hit was not of anye Care of
    the Shippe but onelie of a moste Cowardlie
25 mynde of the Master⁷ and Cheefeste of the
    Companye to returne home· / nowe yoᵂ shall
    vnderstande that the Captaine⁸ was verie ⁓
    sicke & synce the tyme that the Shippe

1. This excuse does not appear to be justified, as the roadstead off the mouth of the entrance to Espírito Santo is not now noted for any difficulties in providing anchorage.

2. "that" deleted after "howe."

3. "go" inserted after "woulde."

4. The Canal de Sebastião offers safe and roomy anchorage, entered at lat. 23° 43′ S, long. 45° 24′ from the north, between Ilha de São Sebastião and the mainland. *South America Pilot,* part 1 (1945), pp. 279–80.

5. "businesses." Purchas, *Pilgrimes* 4:1198.

6. "there make." Ibid.

7. Again possibly Robert Tharlton, but see p. 106 below.

8. Captain John Cocke.

It came for my onelie intention was to gett
out of that badd rode & to put of into the
sea & there to determyne what to doe, for
that place was not for us to tarie in, for the
rode was so badde as wee were not able to
helpe our selues in a bootes ladinge of the
water wch great wee stoode in noe smalle
wante of: in this dayes staye in the rode I
comforted these distressed more then what
I mighte, and I founde moste of theire
desire to returne againe into Englande /
I lett them understande here that wee
woulde barke againe to the Ilande of Saynt
Sabastion, and there wee woulde water &
doe our othere necessarie busines. and there
to make a resolute determination of the
reste of our proseedinge. this sowr he
somed to like them all verie well, but the
companye in the rockinke instantelie
desired nothinge more then to returne
home, all affirminge that it was pittie
since a shippe should be caste of, but
in trueth it was not of any care of
the shippe but onelie of a moste cowardlie
mynde of the mon & theefeste of the
companye to returne home / nowe yu shall
understande that the captaine was here
sicke & shynie he by me that the shippe

1   Loste hir mastes shee became the moste ⁓ ⁓
    laborsome shipp that ever did swyme in ⁓
    the sea so as hee was not able to indure in
    her · & at that present laye a borde my shippe
5   so as theire was non of anye truste¹ or ⁓
    accompte lefte in her· / but souche was the
    case² of that shippe beinge withowt sailes
    mastes or anye manner of tackle as in
    the sence & Iudgemente of anye man
10 liveinge there did not live that desperate
    minded men in the worlde which in that
    case³ she was then in woulde haue ventered
    to haue sayled in her half so farre as ⁓
    Englande, and if shee doe returne hit
15 is in my opinion the most admirable
    returne that ever shippe made,⁴ being so
    farre of & in her case⁵ / these villaynes
    haveinge lefte in my shippe all their hurte
    men, & haveinge aborde of them both the
20 surgeons,⁶ I haueinge not one in my owne
    Shippe which did knowe howe to laye a ⁓
    plaster to a wounde much lesse to Cure
    anye by salues / & further they having
    in theire shippe three tymes the proportion
25 of my vittaile wherein Consisted the oneli
    Relefe & Comforte of all my Companye, ⁓
    these moste harde harted villaynes ⁓
    determined that nighte amongste them
    selues to lose me at there next convenient
30 tyme the Could espye · & in this case

1. Altered from "not anye of truste."

2. "cause" altered to "case."

3. "cause" deleted; "case" inserted.

4. Yet the *Roebuck* returned safely, and we have
no evidence that she was in particularly bad shape
when she arrived in England.

5. "cause" altered to "case."

6. One of the surgeons claimed to be a faith-
healer who "cured by words" (Purchas *Pilgrimes*
4:1205). One may well have been Thomas
Lodge, the writer, who was afterwards to take his
M.D. and may have had some experience as
a ship's surgeon behind him. The indications,
such as they are, are that he was on the *Roebuck*.

Loste thir master sehe became the most
laborsome shipp that ever did swymme in
the sea so as she was not able to endure in
her, at that present laye aborde my shippe
s6 as there was none of anye of trust or
accompte lefte in her, but soe was the
cause of that shippe beinge without sailer
master or anye manner of tackle as in
the sence & judgemente of any man
lyvinge there did not live that desperate
minded men in the worlde we in that
case she was then in woulde have ventured
to have sayled in her halfe so farre as
Englande, and if she too retourne hit
is in my opinion the moste admirable
returne that ever shippe made, beinge so
farre of & in her case / these villaynes
havinge lefte in my shippe all their hurte
men, & havinge aborde of them bothe the
surgeons, & leavinge not one in my owne
shippe wch did knowe howe to laye a
plaster to a wounde muche lesse to cure
anye by salves, & further they havinge
in their shippe the very true proportion
of my vittaile wch therin consisted the onely
relefe & comforte of all my company, &
these moste hard harted villaynes
determined that nighte amongste them
selves to loose me at their next convenient
tyme they could espye. & in this case

1   To goe for Englande, leaveinge vs in the moste[1] greatest
     distres that euer one christian lefte a nothere
     in.[2] for wee had all her hurte men in vs, and we
     had taken owt of hir the beste parte of her
5   men not longe before,[3] so as in runinge from
     vs the not onelie Caried awaye our surgons
     & all their provision, but also the vittaile
     where in consisted all our Relefe and Comforte
     haveinge in them at theire departure but
10   46. men · Carieinge awaye with them the ~
     proportion for 6 monethes vittaile for 120 men
     at lardge[4] / I leaue you to Consider of this part
     of theires & the miserable case[5] I was lefte
     in with so manye hurte men so fewe vittaile[6]
15   & my bote beinge so badde as 6 or 7 men ~
     Continuallye baylinge water, were scante
     able to kepe hir from sinckeing. & mend hir
     wee coulde by[7] noe meanes[8] before we
     recovered some shore / for had not these ~
20   villaynes[9] in the Roobucke that
     nighte we Roode in this Baye suffered their
     Bote to Run a shore with Irishe men[10] which
     went a shore to betraye vs, I had taken hir
     Bote & suncke this greate naughtie bote,
25   such was the greatenes of our mishappes
     as wee were not lefte with the Comforte
     & hope of a bote to releue our selues withall
     wee not haueinge lefte in the[11] shipp not 3[12]
     tunes of water for a 140 men the moste
30   whereof[13] beinge hurte and sicke ~

1. "moste" inserted; omitted Purchas, *Pilgrimes*
4:1198.
2. Was the master of the *Roebuck* Robert Tharlton? Richard Hawkins said he deserted him in
1593 off the Río de la Plata, as he, when with
Cavendish, "forsooke his Fleete, his Generall and
Captaine, and returned home" (*Observations*,
ed. J. A. Williamson, pp. 69–70). This might
point to him as the master of the *Daintie*, since
her captain was not on board when she deserted
and presumably her master took her home. If
this is so, the *Daintie* survived to return to
England. But it is possible Richard Hawkins was
mistaken in the circumstances, and that the
desertion referred to was that of the *Roebuck*,
with Tharlton as her master.

3. Knivet (Purchas 4:1206) says that when they
arrived at Ilha de São Sebastião, it was intended
to burn one of the ships, consolidate the resources
of the other with her men and equipment, and
return to the Strait of Magellan. To him this
constituted the grounds for the desertion of the
Roebuck: "the company that was in the Roebucke, hearing of it, in the night runne away
from vs, and we left alone againe."
4. If Cavendish's allegation that the *Roebuck*
had victuals for 120 men for six months is
correct, then it is clear that between them the two
vessels had victuals for their 186 men for four
months at least so that they could, if Cavendish
had not been so obstinate, have safely returned
to England.

To goe for Englande, leaveinge vs in the greatest distres that ever one christian lefte a nother, ffor wee had all ye Irishe men in vs, and wee had taken out of hir the beste parte of hir men not longe before, but in runinge from vs, they not onelie caried away our surgeons & all their provision, but also the vittailes wherein consisted all our releefe and comforte they haveinge with them at their departure but 46. men carrienge away in them the proportion for 6 monethes vittailes for 120 men at large, I leave you to consider of their part of theirs & the miserable case I was lefte in with so many hurte men so fewe vittailes & my bote beinge so badde as 6 or 7 men continually bayeinge water, were scante able to keepe hir from sinckinge; mend hir wee coulde by noe meanes before wee recovered some shore; ffor had not those villaynes in the roobote that night wee roode in this baye suffered their bote to runn a shore & so the Irishe men that went a shore to betraye vs, & so had taken hir roote, I thincke hir greate daunger bote, since was the greateneß of our mishappes as wee were not lefte w[i]th the comforte & hope of a bote to releeve our selves w[i]th all wee not haveinge lefte in pr̄ ship not 3 tunnes of water for a 140 men the moste wherof beinge hurte and sicke.

---

5. "cause" deleted; "case" inserted.

6. "so little victuall." Purchas 4:1198.

7. "not" deleted before "by."

8. "mend her we could not by any meanes."
Purchas 4:1198.

9. "that nighte" deleted after "villaynes."

10. "to run ashore with Irish men (which went
to betray vs)." Purchas 4:1198.

11. "our" deleted: "the" inserted.

12. "scarce three." Purchas 4:1198.

13. "the most part whereof." Ibid.

1   Wee putinge owt of the Roode the next daie, they
    the same nighte, in this case¹ lefte vs, & as I ⁓
    suppose they coulde not accompte otherwise, then
    that wee shoulde neuer agayne be harde on,² the
5   next morninge lokeinge for the Roobucke shee ⁓
    Coulde noe where be seene / I leue to yoᵂ to Iudge
    in what plighte my Companye was in,³ being
    nowe destitute of surgons vittailes & all other ⁓
    Relefe which in truthe was so greate a discomforte
10 vnto them, as they held them selues as deade
    men as well whole as hurte, the scantnes of ⁓
    water made vs that we coulde not seeke after
    them but were inforced to seeke to this Iland⁴
    with all possible speede haveinge to beate backe
15 againe thither 200 leagues which place god suffered
    vs to gette, with our laste Caske water· the ⁓
    poore men beinge moste extremelie pynched
    by wante⁵ thereof where after wee had a litle
    refreshed our selues wee presentlie mended our
20 Bote in such sorte as with greate labor & ⁓
    dannger we broughte 40 tunes of water a borde,
    & in the meane tyme searcheinge our store
    of Ropes tackle and sayles, we founde our ⁓
    selues vtterlie vnfurnished bothe of Ropes &
25 sayles which accident pleased the Companye
    not a little, for by these wantes they assuredli
    accompted to goe whome,⁶ then makeinge a
    survaye of the vittaile wee found to be ⁓
    Remayneinge in the Shippe accordeing to the
30 Rate wee then lived at 14 wiekes vittayles
    lardge / haveinge Rigged our shippes in such
    sorte as our smale store woulde furnishe vs

1. "cause" altered to "case."   4. Ilha de São Sebastião.
2. "heard of." Purchas, *Pilgrimes* 4:1198.   5. "for want." Purchas 4:1198.
3. "in" omitted. Ibid.   6. Replaced by "home." Ibid.

in dep~tinge out of the Road the next daie, the
the same nighte, in there came lettr &c, as I
suppose they could not accomplishe ther viag~, then
that wee shuld neuer againe be heard on, the
next mornynge lokeinge for the roobuke we
could noe wheare be seene, I leaue to yo~ to Judge
in what plighte my Company~ was in, beinge
nowe destitute of surgeon~ vittailes & all of o~
releefe w~ch trulie was so greate a discomforte
vnto them, as they held them selues as dead~
men as well might as hurte, the scantnes of
water made vs that we could not seeke after
them but were inforced to seeke to this Iland
w~th all possible speede, haueinge to beate backe
againe thither 200 leagues w~ch place god suffered
vs to gette, w~th our laste dashe water, the
poore men beinge muste extremelie oppressed
by wante thereof, w~ch after wee had a litle
refreshed our selues wee presentlie moured our
Boate in suche sorte as w~th greate labor &
daunger we brought 40 tunnes of water aboard,
& in the meane tyme tarryenge our store
of w~ched tackle and sayles, we founde our
selues vtterlie vnfurnished bothe of w~ches &
sayles w~ch aardent pleased the company~
not a litle, for by thes wantes we, as finallie
acompted to goe w~home, then makeinge a
surbayes of the vittaile w~ch founde to be
remayninge in L~p shippes acordinge to the
rate wee then liued at w~ was weekes vittailes
largelye, haueinge hurg of our shippes in suche
sorte as our smale store would furnish the~

1 Which was moste maynelie,¹ for we had but 4
sayles our spritte sayle & foretoppe sayle² being
wanteinge, which two the shippe moste principallye loueth,³ & those which wee had (except
5 hir mayne saile) were more then half worne
in this poore case beinge furnished & our water
beinge taken in, my Companye knowinge
my determination which was to hale⁴ my bote
a ground & buylde her neewe·⁵ / they fourthwith
10 openlie begane to murmer & muten,⁶ affirming
plainelie that I neede not mende the bote,
for they woulde goe home & then there ⁓
shoulde be noe vse of hir, I heareinge these
speaches thoughte hit was nowe tyme
15 to loke amongste them, Called them together
& telled⁷ them that althoughe wee had many
mishappes fallen vppon vs, yet I hoped
that there myndes woulde not in such sorte
be overcome· with anye of these misfortunes
20 that they woulde goe abowt to vndertake ⁓
anye base or disordered Course but that they would
cheerefulli⁸ goe forewarde to atempte ether
to make them selues famous in resalutelie
dyeinge, or in liveinge to performe that which
25 wilbe to theire perpetuall reputations·⁹ &
telled¹⁰ them the more wee attempted beinge
in so weke a case,¹¹ the more if wee ⁓
performed woulde be to our honours, but ⁓
Contrarie wise if wee dyed in¹² atempeing
30 wee did but that which wee Came for, which
was ether to performe or dye / and then

1. "meanely." Purchas, *Pilgrimes* 4:1198.
2. The spritsail was set on a yard extended under the bowsprit; the foretopsail was the third course on the foremast.
3. "lacketh" deleted and "loueth" inserted, in shaky hand; "loueth." Purchas 4:1199.
4. "haile." Ibid. The meaning is haul.
5. "new." Ibid.
6. "mutinie." Ibid.
7. "told." Ibid.
8. "Carefullye" deleted; "cheerefulli" inserted.
9. "reputation." Purchas 4:1199.
10. "telled them" omitted. Ibid.
11. "Cause" deleted; "case" inserted.
12. "not" deleted; "in" inserted.

which was moste marvelie, for wee had but 4
sayles our spritte sayle & foretoppe sayle being
mayntenige, wch two the shippe moste princip=
allye carietts, & thes wch wee had (except
the mayne sayle) were more then halfe worne
in theis poore rase being somewhat rudnelie
beinge taken in, my companye knowinge
my determination wch was to hale my bote
a ground & buylde her newe, they forthwth
openlie begane to murmur & muten, affirming
plainelie that I neede not mende the bote,
for they woulde goe hence & then there
woulde be noe use of hir, I perceivinge theyse
speaches thoughte that it was nowe tyme
to loke amongste them, called them togethor
& tolde them that althoughe wee had many
mischappes fallen uppon us, yet I hoped,
that theire myndes woulde not in suche sorte
be overrunne, wth anye of those misfortunes
that they woulde goe about to undertake
anye base or disordered course but that woulde
carefullie [regretfullie] goe forwarde to atempte ether
to make them selves famous in resolutelie
dyenge, or in livinge to performe that wch
wilbe to theire perpetuall reputation &c,
tolde them the more wee attempted beinge
in so weake a case [state], the more if noe
performed woulde be to our honour, but
contrarie wise if noe dyed not atempeing
wee did but that wch wee came for that
was ether to performe or dye, and theire

1   I shewed them my det*er*minacion to goe againe
     for the straightes of Magalanus[1] w*hi*ch wordes were
     noe sooner vttered but fourthew*i*th they all
     w*ith* one consente affirmed plainelie they woulde
5   never goe that waye againe, and that they would
     all rather staie a shore in that desarte Iland[2]
     then in such case[3] to goe for the straightes
     I soughte by peaceable meanes to p*er*swade them
     showinge them that in goinge that waye wee
10   shoulde releue our vittailes by salteinge of
     sailes[4] & birdes w*hi*ch they did well knowe wee
     mighte doe in greater quantitie, then our
     shippe Coulde Carrie, & furder if wee gotte
     thorrow the straighte,w*hi*ch wee mighte now
15   easelie p*er*forme Consideringe wee had the
     Cheefest parte of som*m*er before vs, wee could
     not but make a moste riche viage and
     also mete againe w*i*th the two smale
     shippes w*hi*ch were gone from vs & that hit
20   was but 600 leagues[5] thither & to goe into
     England they had 2000·[6] and furder that
     they shoulde be moste infamous to the world
     that beinge w*i*thin 600· leagues of the place
     w*hi*ch wee so muche desired,[7] to returne home
25   a gaine so farre, beinge moste infamous
     & beggerlie / these p*er*swacions toke noe ~
     place w*i*th them, but moste boldelie they
     all affirmed that they hadd sworne that
     they woulde neuer goe agayne to the ~
30   straightes, nether by noe meanes would they
     & one of the Chiefest of their faction[8]
     moste proudelie & stubbornelie vttered

1. Cavendish thus continued to demonstrate his determination to adhere to his original course. How sincere he was in expecting his men to accept his propositions is hard to say. By stressing them here he is guarding his reputation for tenacity and courage.

2. The quality of Ilha de São Sebastião, formerly extolled, has now, in his view, suffered a decline.

3. "cawse" altered to "case."

4. "Seales." Purchas 4:1199. On the salting of seal and penguin flesh for food at Puerto San Julián, see Hakluyt, *Principal navigations* 3 (1600):850.

5. He thus reckoned the distance to the Strait from the Ilha de São Sebastião as some 1,800 nautical miles, an appreciable underestimate.

6. His estimate of their distance from England as 6,000 miles was something of an overestimate. He somewhat strains the evidence in the direction he wishes the argument to go.

7. This again was special pleading. The place they desired was not the Strait of Magellan but the Philippines or the coast of China at a vastly farther distance away.

8. The leader of the opposition faction has not been identified.

I shewed them my determination to goe againe
for the straightes of magelaunes, wch wordes were
noe sooner uttered but forthwth they all
wth one consente affirmed plainelie they woulde
never goe that waye againe; and that they woulde
all rather staie ashore in that deserte Jland
then ymshuraise to goe for the straightes
I sought by peaceable meanes to perswade them
shewinge them that in goinge that waye wee
coulde releue our uittailes by saltinge of
saile birdes wch they did well knowe wee
might doe in greater quantitie, then our
shippe coulde carrie, and furder if wee gotte
thorrowe the straightes, wch wee might wth
easelie performe consideringe wee had the
choppest parte of somer before us, wee could
not but make a moste riche uiage, and
well moste againe only the two smale
shippes wch were gone from us, that that
was but 600 leagues thither, to goe into
England they had 2000 and furder that
they shoulde be moste infamous to the world
that beinge wthin 600 leagues of the place
where wee so muche desired; to returne home
againe so barre, beinge moste infamous
and beggerlie, these perswations tooke noe
place wth them, but moste boldelie they
all affirmed that they had sworne that
they woulde never goe againe to the
straightes, neither by noe meanes woulde they
and one of the cheifest of their faction
moste proudelie and stubbornelie uttered

1   Theise wordes to my face in presence of all the
     reste, which I seeinge & fyndeinge my owne ⁓
     faction to be so weake for their were not any
     that favered my parte but my poore Coussen
5   Cocke¹ & the m*aste*r of the Shippe,² I toke this
     boulde Companion by the bosome & w*i*th my
     owne handes put a Rope abowt his necke
     meaneinge resolutelie to strangle him for
     weapon abowt me I had none³ / his Companions
10   seinge one of their Cheif Champions in this
     case⁴ & p*er*ceiveinge me to goe roundelie to ⁓
     worke w*i*th him they all⁵ Came to the m*aste*r & ⁓
     desired him to speake, affirminge they ⁓
     would be Redye to take anye course that I
15   should thincke goode of· / I heareinge of
     this staied my self & let the fellowe goe
     after w*hi*ch tyme I found them some thing
     Conformable at leaste in speaches· thoughe
     a monge them selues they still murmured at
20   my intentions· thus haveing some thing
     pascified them & p*er*swaded them, that by noe
     meanes I woulde take anye other course:
     then to goe for the straightes· / I toke a shore
     w*i*th me 30 souldiers & my Carpenters⁶ Carieng
25   14 daies vittailes w*i*th me for them, thus
     goinge a shore I halled⁷ vppe my Boote to
     neewe buyld her⁸ in suche sorte as shee ⁓
     might be able to abide the seaes, leveing
     A borde all my saileres & the Rest to Rigge the
30   Shippe & mend sailes & to do other busines

1. Purchas (*Pilgrimes* 4:1199 and elsewhere) gives Captain John Cocke's name as "Locke." This may simply be a printing or copying error, though it may result from a mistaken identification, "Cocke" being correct.

2. Steven Seaver, it would appear.

3. Cavendish clearly gave way to his temper in this instance and his action can scarcely be regarded as simply disciplinary.

4. "cause" deleted; "case" inserted.

5. "all" inserted in a shaky hand.

6. Cavendish also took some twenty more or less moribund men ashore with him and left them, Anthony Knivet tells us, to shift for themselves. Purchas 4:1206.

7. "hailed." Purchas 4:1199.

8. Cavendish would need to make a sawpit to cut planking and would also probably require a forge to make nails.

Theise wordes to my fare in presence of all the
reste, which I showinge & shewinge my owne
faction to be so weake for there were not any
that favered my parte but my poore donnou-
torke & the m of the Shipp, I toke this
bonde companion by the bosime with my
owne handes put a rope about his necke
meaninge resolutelie to straungle him the
weapon about me I had none his companions
beinge one of theyr cheif champions in this
case & perswadinge me to goe roundelie to
worke with him & they dewne to the me
desired him to speake, affirminge they
would be redye to take anye course that I
should thincke good of. I hearinge of
this staied my selfe & let the follwe goe
after with tyme I found them some thing
conformable at leaste in speache thoughe
amonge them selues they still murmured at
my intentions. this havinge bine this
gastified them & perswaded them, that by no
meanes I would take anye other course
then to goe for the straughter, I to be assere
with me 30 souldiers & my darpouters carieinge
it daies vittailes with me for them, thus
goinge a shore I called uppe my Booke to
nowe buyld or in suche sorte as she
might be able to abide the seas, reberinge
a borde all my sailers & the rest to trygge the
Shipp & mend sailes & to do other busines

1 And nowe to let yo^w knowe in what case[1] I laye
  a shore amonge these base men. you shall ～
  vnderstand that of these 30 their were verie
  fewe of them which had not rather haue gonne
5 to the Portingales then to haue remained with
  me, for there were some, which at my being
  a shore were makeinge Rafes[2] to goe over to
  the mayne, which was not A mile over
  where the Portingales had continuall watch
10 of vs, lokeinge but for a fitte oportunitie to set
  vppon vs / beinge in this case[3] alwaies ～
  expectinge the cominge of the Portingales
  againste whome I could haue made smale[4] ～
  Resistance, and further the trecherie of
15 some of my Companye which desired nothing
  more then to steale over so to betraye me
  I protest I liued howerlie as hee that
  still expecteth deathe, in this case[5] I
  made all the speede I coulde to make an end
20 of my Bote that wee mighte be able to Rowe her
  a borde which in 12 dayes wee maynelie finished
  which beinge downe· I Came a borde & found all
  my busines in goode forwardenes, so I ～
  determined with all possible speede to despatch
25 & be gone for the straightes of Magalane,
  But or euer wee Could gett in all our water
  & tymber woode[6] and other necessaries, An
  Irishe man a noble villaigne haveinge made
  a Rafe,[7] gotte ouer to the mayne & telled the
30 Portingales which were there watcheing
  nothinge but an oportunitie,[8] that if they

1. "cause" deleted; "case" inserted.
2. "rafts." Purchas, *Pilgrimes* 4:1199.
3. "cause" deleted; "case" inserted.
4. "made no." Purchas 4:1199.
5. "cause" deleted; "case" inserted.
6. "Timber-wood." Purchas 4:1199. It is more probable that Cavendish meant to write "tymber, woode," timber being planking necessary for repairs and wood being firewood for the ship's galley.

7. "raft." Ibid. The Irish element on board, on which we have no information, may have had some cooperation from English Catholics among the ship's company.

8. The local Portuguese captain, Salvador de Correa, had sent up and down the coast for reinforcements. A number had arrived by this time from Río de Janeiro under the command of Martím Correia de Sá. Knivet, *Vária Fortuna,* p. 40n; Purchas 4:1207.

And nowe to let yo knowe in what I layd
before amonge these base men, you shall
understand that of these 30 loytermore serv-
ants of leom were, had not rather have gone
to the portingales then to have remained with
me, for there were some, with at my being
a shore were makinge rafes to goe over to
the mayne, with was not a mile over
where the portingales had continuall watch
of vs, lokinge but for a fitte oportunitie to set
vppon vs, beinge in this case alwaies
expectinge the cominge of the portingales
against whome I could have made smale
resistance, and seeinge the treacherie of
some of my companye with desired nothing
more then to steale over & to betraye me
I protest I lived tediouslie & as god that
stirr oportolith doath, in this case I
made all the speede I could to make an end
of my Noate that me might be able to vse or
aborde with in 12 daies was maynelie finished
Our beinge downe & have aborde & stowed all
my busines in goode forwardnes, I &
determined with all possible speede to dispatch
& be gone for the straightes of magalane,
But or ever we could gett in all our water
& tymber woode and other necessaries, an
Irishe man a noble villaine havinge made
a rafe, gotte over to the mayne & tolled the
portugales with were there watchinge
nothinge but an oportunitie, that if they

1 Woulde goe over in the nighte they shoulde ～
  fynde moste of our men a shore w*i*thowte ～
  weapon· & that they mighte doe by theym
  what they woulde· / Vppon this they the next
5 nighte Came over[1] & haveinge taken some of our
  men, they broughte them where they rest[2]
  laye, w*i*ch they moste Cruellye killed, the
  moste beinge sicke men[3] not being able to
  sturre to helpe them selues, those w*i*ch[4] were
10 a shore more then the sicke men had stollen
  owt of the shippe, for hit was all my Care
  to kepe them A borde knoweinge well that
  they Portingales[5] soughte to spoyle vs, the ～
  place beinge so fitte for them,[6] w*i*ch was all
15 over growen w*i*th woodes & busshes· as their
  Indians mighte goe & spoyle vs w*i*th their
  Arrowes at theire pleasure[7] And wee not
  be able to hurte one of them· / in the morning
  p*er*ceaveinge their Cominge I sent my boote
20 A shore & rescued all my helthefull men
  but fyve[8] / w*i*ch they found owt in the night
  w*i*thowt weapons to defend them, wherof
  beside the losse of our men, wee haveing
  but 4 sailes loste one[9] a shore w*i*ch was noe
25 smale mishappe amonge the reste· /
  The Portingales went p*re*sentlie againe
  over to the mayne, but lefte their Indians
  to kepe in the busshes A bowt the watering
  place,[10] our men going A shore were[11]
30 shotte at & hurte & Could by noe meanes

1. "vpon this, the next night, they came ouer."
Purchas, *Pilgrimes* 4:1199.
2. "the rest." Ibid.
3. "killed, being sicke men." Ibid.
4. "w*i*ch" inserted in a shaky hand.
5. "the Portugals." Purchas 4:1199.
6. "which was" omitted. Ibid.

7. "pleasures." Ibid.
8. The unfit men were left to their own devices,
Knivet among them. Purchas 4:1207.
9. "left one." Ibid., p. 1200.
10. "bushes. About the watering-place, our
men." Ibid.
11. "sh" crossed out at the end of the line.

woulde goe over in the night they shoulde
fynde moste of our men a shore w{th}oute
weaponse, that they might doe by theyr
what they woulde. / vppon this they the next
nyghte came over & havinge taken some of our
men, they broughte to them where they hest
laye, w{th} they moste cruellye killed, they
moste beinge sicke men not being able to
sturre to helpe them selves, they w{th}drewe
a shore more then they sicke men had stollen
out of the shipp, for hit was all my care
to keepe them aborde knowinge well that
they portingales soughte to spoyle us, the
place beinge so fitte for them, but so are we
over growen w{th} woodes that theyr at theyr
Indians mighte goe & spoyle us w{th} theyr
arrowes att theyr pleasure and wee not
be able to hurte one of them, in the morning
pceavinge theyr comminge I sent my boate
a shore & resqued all my helthefull men
but fyve, w{th} they founde out in the night
w{th}out weapons to defend them, w{th}out
besydes the losse of our men, wee havinge
but 4 sailes loste one a shore w{th} was noe
smale mischeepe amonge the reste. /
& the portingales went psentelie againe
over to the mayne, but lefte theyr Indians
to keepe in the bushes & bolde the wateringe
place, our men going & shore wer so
shotte at & hurte & coulde by noe meanes

1   Come to hurte them againe by reason of the wood
and busshes, wherefore fyndeinge my men ∽
hurte & that by any[1] meanes I coulde doe[2]
nothinge there withowte more lose of men

5   which[3] I had noe neede of, for I had not lefte above
90· men or little over, I notwithstandinge my[4] wantes
of[5] woode & water & my bote beinge not ∽
sufficientlie mended was in noe possibilitie to
doe me pleasure, in this case[6] was I forced to

10 departe, fortune neuer ceaseinge to laye her
greateste aduersities vppon me / but nowe I
am growne so weake & fainte as I am scarce
able to holde the penn in my hande, Wherefore
I muste leue you to inquire of the reste of

15 our moste vnhappie proseedeinges: / but ∽
knowe this that for the straightes I could
by noe meanes get my Companie to giue
their Consentes to goe, for after this ∽
misfortune and the wante of our sayles

20 which was a chief matter, they alleaged
& to tell you truthe all the men lefte in the[7]
shippe were noe more then[8] able to waye our
Ankors / but in truthe I desired nothing more
then to attempte that course rather desireinge

25 to dye in goinge forwarde then baselie in ∽
Returneinge backeward againe / but god ∽
woulde not suffer me to dye so happye a man
althoughe I sought all the wayes I could
still to atempte to performe some what, for

30 after that[9] by noe meanes I see[10] they coulde
be brought to goe for the straightes haveing

---

1. "noe" deleted; "any" inserted.
2. "no" deleted.
3. "whereof." Purchas, *Pilgrimes* 4:1200.
4. "not aboue ninetie men left, or little ouer, notwithstanding." Ibid.
5. Four minims crossed out before "of."

6. "cause" deleted; "case" inserted.
7. "our" deleted; "the" inserted.
8. "then" inserted.
9. "I see" deleted.
10. "I see" inserted; "I saw." Purchas 4:1200.

come to hurte them againe by reason of the mud
and bushes, wherefore vnderstandinge my men
hurte & that by ann meanes I coulde doe me
not hurte there in I coulde more losse of men
wch I had noe neede of, for I had not loste aboue
90. men or little ouer, I notwithstandinge my wounde
in of mudd & water & my bote beinge not
sufficientlie mended was in noe possibilitie to
doe me pleasure, in this was I forced to
departe, fortune neuer ceasinge to laye her
greatest aduersitids vppon me / but now I
am growne so weake & fainte as I am scarce
able to hold the penn in my hande, wherefore
I muste leaue you to inquire of the reste of
our moste vnhappie proceedinges / But
knowe this that for the straightd I would
by noe meanes yet my companie to giue
their consent to goe, for after this
misfortune and the wante of our sayles
wch was a spoil matter, they alleaged
to tell you truthe all the men loste in the
shippe were noe more able to maye our
anckers, but in truthe I desired nothing more
then to attempte that rome so rather desiringe
to dye in goinge forwarde then basely in
returninge backward againe, but god
woulde not suffer me to dye so happye a man
although I sought all the wayes I could
still to attempte to proceed some what, for
after that I see by noe meanes they could
be brought to goe for the straightd labor

1   so manye reasonable occasions to alleage againste m[e]
     as they had, firste haveinge but 3 sayles and the
     place subiect to such furiouse stormes & the lose
     of one of these was deathe, & furthere our bote
5   was not suffieientlie repaired to abide the ⁓
     seaes, and laste of all the fewnes and wekenes
     of our Companye wherein wee had not lefte ⁓
     30 sailers, these causes beinge alleaged Against
     me I, coulde not well annswere, but I ⁓
10   Resolued them playnelie that to[1] England I ⁓
     woulde neuer giue my consent to goe, and
     that if they woulde not take such Courses as
     I entended, that then I was determined that
     shippe and all shoulde sincke in the seaes
15   togethere· / Vppon this they begane to be more
     tractable & then I shewed them that I ⁓
     woulde beate for *Sainte Elena*·[2] / And there
     ethere to make our selffes happie by mending
     or endinge· / This course in truthe pleased
20   none of them· & yet seeinge my determinacion
     & supposeinge hit woulde be more daunger to
     Resiste me then in seemeinge to be willing,
     they were at quyet, vntill I had beaten ⁓
     from 29 degrees to the southewarde of the
25   equator[3] to 20[4] at which tyme I fyndin[g]
     that I was to farre northerlie to haue
     goode wynde, I called them to tacke abowt
     the Shippe to the southewarde Againe
     they all plainelie made Annswere the
30   would not & that they had rather dye
     there then be starued in seekeing a[n]

1. "to" inserted.
2. St. Helena lies at lat. 15° 58′ S, long. 5° 43′ W. Cavendish's own chart (pl. 7) shows the island at approximately the correct latitude, but somewhat to the east of its true position.
3. "quarter" deleted before "equator."
4. Cavendish needed to be rather farther from the Brazilian coast at lat. 20° S, unless he could sail to some extent into the wind, which his defective rigging and sails would not, it appears, permit him to do. Otherwise the SE Trades would carry him back to the northeast coast of Brazil. Sailing to 29° S would not help him unless he could make an appreciable easting before or as he turned northward again.

so many reasonable occasions to alleage against me
as they had, christe knoweinge but 3 saylers and the
place subiect to these furious stormes, the losse
of one of these was teachd, and that our bote
was not suffitioutlie repaired to abide the
seate, and laste of all the sicknes and weloned
of our company whereie wee had not lefte
30 saylers, these causes beinge alleaged against
me, I could not well answere, but I
resolued them playnelie that England I
should neuer giue my consent to goe, and
that if they would not take such courses as
I entended, that then I was determined that
shippe and all should sincke in the seas
togethere. wppon this they began to be more
tractable. c then I sesmed them that I
would beate for Sainte Elena. and here
I they to make our selfes happie by mending
or endinge. this course wichnthy pleasd
none of them. yet seeinge my determination
c supposeinge that would be more daunger to
resiste me then in somewhat to be willinge,
they were at quyet, butill I had beaten
from 29 degrees to the southewarde of the
quarter equator to 20 at which tyme Syndinge
that I was to farre northerlie to haue
goode wynde, I called them to tacke about
the shippe to the southwarde againe
they all playnelie made answere they
would not c that they had rather dye
theie then be starued in seekinge the

1   Ilande[1] w*h*ich they thoughte that waye wee ~
     shoulde never get, what meanes I vsed to
     to[2] stand againe to the southeward I leve yo^w[3] to inquir[e]
     of them selues, but from the latitude of 20 I
5   beate backe againe into 28 w*i*th such ~
     contrarye wyndes[4] as I suppose neuer man
     was trobled w*i*th the like so longe a tyme
     togethere, beinge in this latitude I found
     the winde fauorable & then I stoode againe
10   to the northeward willinge the M*aste*r and
     his Companye to sayle east northe east[5]
     & they in the nighte (I beinge a sleepe) stered
     northe easte & meere northerlie,[6] wit*with*stand[e]
     ing all this moste vyle vsage wee gotte
15   w*i*thin 60 leagues of the Iland[7] & had the winde
     fauored vs so as that wee mighte haue stemmed[8]
     from 18 degrees to 16 east northe easte wee
     had founde the Ilande[9] but it was not god*e*s
     will so greate a blessinge should befale me· /
20   beinge nowe in the latitude of the Iland ~
     almoste 80 leagues[10] to the westewarde of hit
     the winde beinge continuallye at east southe
     Easte the moste contrariest[11] wynd that could
     blowe,[12] I p*r*esentlie made a s*u*rvaye of my vittayle
25   & found that according to that proportion[13] of
     vittaile w*h*ich wee then lived at there was
     not lefte in the Shippe 8 wiekes vittaile
     w*h*ich being so farre from Relefe was as I ~
     suppose As smale A portion as euer men
30   were At in the seaes being so vncerten of

1. St. Helena.
2. "get abowt" deleted before "to"; "stand againe to" inserted.
3. "to" deleted before "yo^w."
4. He had come out of the SE Trades into the northerly and westerly winds of the South Atlantic high pressure system. The effect of these winds may well have been enhanced by a tropical storm from a northerly direction.
5. This should have brought him into the belt of the SE Trades and enabled him, if his course was correct, to reach St. Helena (though his estimate of the island's longitude may well have been at fault).
6. From ENE to NE is a change of course from 67° 30′ to 45°; it may be that the whole phrase "northe easte & meere northerlie" is equivalent to NE by N, which is 33° 45′, though "meere northerlie" may be only a rough approximation for some indefinite trend farther north than NE.

7. If his estimate is correct his position would be roughly lat. 16° 20′ S, long. 7° 40′ W.
8. "Stemmed" here means to keep a fixed course.
9. If his estimate is approximately correct his distance from the island would have been in the region of 600 nautical miles.
10. "eighteene leagues." Purchas, *Pilgrimes* 4:1200: this is likely to have resulted from a mistaken copy of "18" for "80" in the manuscript. It would give an estimated position of about lat. 16° S, long. 9° 50 W.
11. "most contrarie." Purchas 4:1200.
12. Such a wind would have meant, from his position, sailing directly into the wind, which would be impossible.
13. "that proportion." Purchas 4:1200.

Ilande wch they thoughte that way^e we
coulde never get, w^t meanes I vsed to get
aboute to the eastward I leue to yo^w to inquire
of the owne Clewes, but from the latitude of 20 I
boate barke againe into 28 wth suche
contrarye wyndes as I suppose neuer man
was trobled mth the like so longe a tyme
togethere, beinge in theis latitude I found
the windes fauorable then I stoode againe
to the norwestward willinge the m^r and
the Companye to beate sayle east northeast
the m^r in the myste (Beinge a sloope) stered
northeaste & moore northerlie, notwithstanding all theis moste vyle wsage wee gotte
wthin 60 leagnes of the Ilande & then the windes
fauored vs so as wee myste haue stemmed
from 18 degrees to 16 east northeaste wee
had synede the Ilande but yt was not gods
wille so greate a blessinge shuld befale me
beinge nowe in the latitude of theis Iland
almoste 80 leagnes to the westward of it
the windes beinge continnally & at east sse the
easte the moste contariest wynd that route
blowe, I presentlie made a suruaye of my vittayle
& founnd that accordinge to that proportion of
vittaile wee wee then liued at there may was
not lefte in the shippe 8 wioles vittaile
ours beinge so farre from releefe was as I
suppose as smale a proportion as euer men
were at in the suche beinge so vnerten y^t

1   Relefe, I demaunded of them whether they woulde
     venture like goode minded men to beate to the
     southewarde againe to get this Iland, where
     wee shoulde not onelie releue our selues but also be
5   in full assurance ethere to sincke or take a
     Carracke·¹ / & that by this meanes wee should
     haue A sufficient revenge of the Portingal[es]
     for all their villanyes donne vnto vs, or that
     they woulde pynche & bate half the allowance
10   they had before & so to goe for England, they
     all annswered me the woulde pynche to death
     rather then goe againe to the Southeward·² /
     I knowinge their dispositions & haueinge liued
     amongst them in such continuall tormente
15   & disquitenes, and nowe to tell yoᵘ of my
     greatest greef which was the sickenes of my
     deare kynsman Iohn Cock³ whoe by this
     tyme was growne in greate weaknes by
     Reason whereof hee desired rather quietnes
20   and Contentednes in our Course, then such
     continuall disquietnes which never ceassed me
     & nowe by this what with greif for hym &
     the Continuall troble I indewred amongst
     such hel houndes · my spirit was⁴ Cleene spent
25   wishinge my self vppon any desarte place
     in the worlde there to dye, rather then
     thus basely to returne home agayne· / which
     Course I had put in execution, had I found
     an Iland which the Cartes make to be in 8
30   degrees to the southeward of the lyne,⁵ I

1. As already indicated St. Helena lay on the
track of and was a calling place for the carracks
of the *Carreira da Índia* from Goa to Lisbon.
2. "goe to the Southward againe." Purchas,
Pilgrimes 4:1200.
3. Captain John Cocke, Purchas again (4:1200)
printing "Locke."

4. "my Spirits were." Purchas 4:1200.
5. The island was Ascension, lat. 7° 57′ S, long.
14° 22′ W. Its position was given with some
approach to accuracy in Cavendish's own chart
(pl. 7).

3

before, I demaunded of them whether they woulde
venture like good minded men to beate to the
southwardes againe to get this Island, wherevppon
wee resolued not onely to renew our selues but also
in still assurance of our to shirke or take a
Carracke, & that by this meanes wee shoulde
haue a sufficient reuenge of the Portingalls
for all their villanyes donne vntovs, or that
they woulde expresse bate that the allowance
they had before is to goe for England, they
all answered mee they woulde expresse to day
rather then goe againe to the Southward.
I finding their dispositions & knowinge liued
amongst them in such continuall tormoute
& disquietnes, and now to take vp of my
greatest greef, which was the sickenes of my
deare kynsman John Cocke, who by this
tyme was growne in y[e] estate weakened by
reason wherof god desired rather ymmediate
a true contentednes in one hour, then this
continuall disquietnes w[ch] never reasoninge
& now by this weate with greif or tyme
the continuall troble I indured amongst
this god confused, my spirit was cleene spent
wishinge my selfe vppon my desarte place
in this worlde then to dye, rather then
thus basely to returne home againe. But
those I had put in execution, god I finde
in Heaven for the hurter made to be in y[e]
daynger to the Southward of the lyne, I

1 Sweare to you I soughte hit w*i*th all diligenc[e]
   meaneinge if I had found hit to haue there
   ended my vnfortunate lief, but god suffered
   noe¹ suche happines to lighte vppon me, for I
5 coulde by noe meanes fynd hit so as I was
   forced to goe towardes England, & haueinge
   gotten 8 degrees² beneathe the lyne I loste my
   moste dearest coussen,³ & now consider wheth[er]
   a harte made of fleshe to be able to indure
10 so manye misfortunes all faleinge vppon
   me w*i*thowt Intermission, I thancke my
   god that in endinge of me he hath pleased
   to Ridde me of all furder troble & misshappes⁴
   And nowe to returne to our private matters
15 I haue made a will,⁵ wherein I haue given
   speciall Chardge that all goodes whatsoeu*er* ∼
   belonges to me to be deliu*e*red into yo*u*r handes·
   for godes sake refuse not to doe this last
   Requeste for me, I owe little that I k[nowe]
20 of & therefore hit wilbe the les troble,
   But if there be anye debte that of ∼
   truthe is owinge by me for godes sake see hit
   paid, I haue lefte a space in the will for ∼
   another name, & if yoʷ thincke hit goode
25 I praye take in my Coussen Henrye ∼
   Sekeforde hee will ease you muche in manye
   businesses⁶ Althoughe hee looke for gaine /
   yoʷ shall fynd hym a verie fitte man in
   some Respectes, to Ioyne w*i*th yoʷ· / there
30 is a byll of adventure to my Coussen ∼

1. "not." Purchas, *Pilgrimes* 4:1201. A pointing finger in margin (see pp. 41–42 above).

2. At this point Cavendish was approximately in the latitude of Ascension Island.

3. We do not know, and cannot even roughly estimate, the date of Captain John Cocke's death.

4. He is here expressing his knowledge that he cannot (or perhaps refuses to) survive for much longer.

5. "my will." Purchas 4:1201. The will, undated, follows on pp. 138–43. A pointing finger in margin.

6. "althoughe" (line 27) through "w*i*th yoʷ" (line 29) omitted in Purchas 4:1201.

care to you & sought to git it with all diligens
& meanewye iff I had founde git to have then
ended my unfortunate lieff, but god suffered
noe such happines to lighte uppon me, for I
coulde by noe meanes fynd git so at I was
forced to goe towardes England, & havinge
gotten ye degrees beneathe the lyne I loste my
moste dearest tenson, & now consider deeply
a harte made of fleshe be able to enduer
so manye misfortunes all fallinge uppon
me wthout intermission I thancke my
god that in endinge of me he hat pleased
to ridde me of all furder troble & mishappes
And nowe to returne to our private matters

B I have made a will, in whom I have given
speciall charge that all goodes what soever
belonger to me to be delivered into yor handes
for goddes sake refuse not to doo this last
requeste of me, I owe little that I knowe
of yf therfore git wilbe the les troble,
But iff there be anye dobte that ost is
truly is owinge by me for goddes sake se git
paid, I have lefte a place in the will for E
an of her name, & iff ye have git goodes
I praye take in my cousson Henrye

Therfore he will ease you muche in many
businesses although he looke for gaine,
yet he hall fynd him a verie fitt man in
some respectes, to Joyne wth ye, se there
is a byll of adventure to my cousou

1   Richarde Cocke¹ if hit happen the othere ship[pe]
    Returne whome wi*t*h anye thinge as hit is [not]²
    Impossible / I praye Remember him for hee
    hathe nothinge to shewe for hit / and likewise
5   M*ast*er Heton the customer of hemton³ which is ～
    50,ₗₗ and one Elliotte of Rettclife by Londo[n]⁴
    w*hi*ch is 50,ₗₗ more the reste haue all billes
    of Adventure but the rune⁵ in the vittaile
    onelie two excepted w*hi*ch I haue written vnto
10 you· / I haue giuen S*ir* George Carie⁶ the
    desier if ever shee Returne for I ～
    always promised hym her if shee ～
    returned and a little parte of her getinge⁷
    If any such thinge happen I praye yoʷ
15 see hit p*er*formed· / to vse Compliment*e*s of loue
    nowe at my laste breathe were frevolus
    But knowe that I lefte none in England
    whome I loued half so well as yo*u*rselfe
    w*hi*ch yoʷ in such sorte deserued at my handes
20 As I Can by noe meanes Requite; I haue left
    all that little Remayninge vnto you not to
    be accomptable for anye thinge· / that w*hi*ch
    you will if yoʷ fynd anye ou*er* plus of Remaynd[er]⁸
    yo*u*r self especiallye beinge satisfied to yo[ur]
25 owne desire, give vnto my sister A[nne]⁹
    Candishe· / I haue written to noo ma[nne]
    but yo*u*r self, leveinge all frindes an[d]
    kynsmen onelie reputeinge you as [dearest]
    Comend me to bothe yo*u*r brothers bei[ng]
30 gladde that yo*u*r brother Edwarde¹⁰ es[caped]

1. Richard Cocke was the younger brother of
Captain John Cocke, and was the second son of
John Cocke of Prittlewell, Essex, and Elizabeth
Wentworth, daughter of Thomas, Lord Went-
worth, and sister to Thomas Cavendish's mother,
who had been Mary Wentworth. *Essex
Archaeological Society Transactions*, 1st ser., 3
(1865):191n, 192; *Miscellanea Genealogica
et Heraldica,* 5th ser., 4 (1935–37):322.
Purchas, *Pilgrimes* 4:1201, has "Richard Locke."

2. The last word in the line is not complete;
"not" is supplied by Purchas 4:1201.

3. Thomas Eaton (Eton or Heton), customer of
Southampton. *Letters of the Fifteenth and*

Sixteenth Centuries, ed. R. C. Anderson,
Southampton Record Society, no. 22 (1921),
pp. 115–16, 178, 215.

4. Elliot of Ratcliffe, Essex, has not been
identified.

5. "ruine." Purchas 4:1201: "they run" is meant.

6. For other provisions relating to whom see
fol. 1v.

7. The *Desire* was presumably handed over to
Carey after she had been brought from Ireland.

8. "has remayned." Purchas 4:1201. The tear in
the margin from here to the bottom of the page
has meant that the lines have had to be completed
from the text in Purchas, though it is not certain

that no changes of wording or spelling were made by him.

9. The surviving letter looks like "D" but is apparently the outer flourish of an "A." Anne is required by the context and by the notes (Appendix II), and is given by Purchas.

10. For Edward Gorges, brother of Tristram, see D. B. Quinn, *The Roanoke Voyages* 1:123, 159, 174, 210, 212; Raymond Gorges, *The Story of a Family* (Boston, 1944), pp. 79–85. The third brother was Sir Arthur Gorges, M.P. (1557–1625). Ibid. pp. 57–78. Pointing fingers in the margin indicate lines 18 and 26 above.

1   So vnfortunate a viage / praye give th[is]
    Copie of my vnhappie proceedeinges in this
    action to none but onelie to *Sir* George Carey
    & tell him that if I had thoughte the letter[s][1]
5   of a deade man woulde haue bynn acceptable
    I woulde haue written vnto him· / I haue
    taken order w*i*th the M*ast*er of my shippe[2] to se[e]
    his peeces of ordinance[3] to be deliu*e*red[4]
    to him, for he knowethe them, and if the
10 Roobucke be not returned, then I haue ⁓
    appointed him to deliver him two brasse ⁓
    peeces owt of this shippe w*hi*ch I praye see
    p*er*formed· / I haue nowe noe more to saye
    but take this laste farewell, that you
15 have loste the loveingest frind that was
    loste by Anye / Comend me to yo*u*r weife[5]
    noe more but as yo^w love god doe not
    Refuse to vndertake this laste Request
    of myne, I praye forget not M*ast*er
20 Carey of Cockington[6] gratifie him w*i*th
    some thinge for he vsed me kindelie at
    my dep*ar*ture,[7] beare w*i*th this scribleinge
    for I protest I am scante able to holde
    A penne in my hand· /[8] ⁓ ⁓
25 *I praye cause to be* ⌐   By him that [most]
    deliuered vnto the | loved you·
    bearer heareof 40^li ⌐   *Thomas C[aundyshe]*[9]
    Th. Caundyshe·

---

1. The word probably read "letters." Purchas (*Pilgrimes* 4:1201) has "letter." Pointing finger in margin, lines 2–3.

2. The master of the *Leicester Galleon* was apparently Steven Seaver.

3. "ordance" deleted.

4. "Ordnance deliuered." Purchas 4:1201.

5. Gorges had married Elizabeth Cole. R. Gorges, *Story of a Family,* pp. 49–53.

6. George Carey of Cockington is usually so called to distinguish him from Sir George Carey of the Isle of Wight. Born about 1541, he was knighted in 1598, and died in 1616. J. L. Vivian, *The Visitations of the County of Devon* (Exeter, 1891), p. 151; W. A. Shaw, *The Knights of England,* 2 vols. (London, 1901), 2:95.

7. George Carey of Cockington had evidently been one of those who bade Cavendish farewell at his departure at Plymouth on 26 August 1591. See Hakluyt, *Principal navigations* 3 (1600): 842.

8. Purchas ends with this line.

9. The last signature is cited in full in the notes attached to the original will: see pp. 42–43. For discussion of the signatures see pp. 3–5 above.

So vnfortunate a viage, I praye yt be the
copie of my vnhappie proceedinges in thes
partes to none but onelie to Sr George Barn
& tell him that iff I had thoughte the lettor
of the deade man woulde haue bynd acceptable
I woulde haue written vnto him. I haue
taken order wth the mr of my shippe to se
his peeces of ordnance ordinaunc to be deliuer
to him, for the knowledge of them, and iff th
roobut be not returned, then I haue
appointed him to deliuer him two brass
peeces owt of his shippe wch I praye be
performed. I haue nowe noe more to saye
but take this laste farewell, that you
haue loste the soveraigest frend that man
loste by anye. Commend me to yo miss
noe more but as yo loue god doe not
refuse to vndertake this laste requeste
of myne, I praye forget not Mr
Darcy of Dorkington, gratifie him wth
some thinge for he vsed me tenderlie at
my departure, beare wth his scribblinge
for I protest I am scante able to gide
the penne in my hand.

I praye cause to be
deliuered vnto the   By him that
bearer heareof 40ti   loved you

Th. Caundyshe   Thomas C

Note — this MS is
printed in the 4ᵗʰ Volume
of Purchas' Pilgrims.
                    Jos: Hunter[1]

1. It has not proved possible to go very far behind this scribbled note by Rev. Joseph Hunter (1783–1861). Sir Thomas Phillipps carried on a correspondence with him and so could have obtained the manuscript before Hunter's death. None of the entries in the posthumous sales (Sotheby's catalogs of 19 December 1861 and 18 June 1862) appears to be the Cavendish one, though Phillipps bought some manuscripts from them. The manuscript was found to be without a number at Sir Thomas Phillipps's death and this was added by Edward Bond when listing a number of manuscripts for probate in 1872. There was a loose slip in the manuscript—"These very curious and valuable." But, though it was probably from a bookseller who handled it at some time, its handwriting has not been identified. Information from Mr. Philip Robinson and Mr. A. N. L. Munby; see also A. N. L. Munby, *The Formation of the Phillipps Library between 1841–1872,* Phillipps Studies no. IV (Cambridge: Cambridge University Press, 1956), pp. 75, 166, 200–201, 207–8.

135

Note — this MS is
printed in the 4th Volume
of Purchas' Pilgrims —

Jos. Hunter

The
Original Will of
Thomas Cavendish

The
Original Will of
Thomas Cavendish

1   In the name of God Amen·[1] This is the last will and
     Testament of me Thomas Caundish being at the making
     hereof in perfect mind and memorye· first I bequeath
     my soule into the handes of Almightie God, my maker,
5   Sauiour, and redemer, by whose death, passion, and
     resurrection I hope to be saued, and to bee an inheritour
     of his heaueanly kingdome. Amen· / ∽ Concerning my
     goodes I dispose of them in maner and forme following. /
     first (if the Roebucke be returned into England)[2] my will
10   is that the saide Roebucke and all such goodes of mine
     as shall be found in her, or haue beene belonging to
     her in whose handes soeuer they shall bee found
     remaining, be deliuered to the handes of Tristram
     Gorge Esquier to be disposed to such vses as this my
15   last will shall import. Also I further will that the
     ship called the Gallion Leicester, with all her goodes
     whatsoeuer to her belonging be deliuered likewise
     to the handes of the saide Tristram Gorge[3]

     Executor to dispose of theese goodes according to this my
20   last will and Testament· I also will that my
     Executors, with speede convenient, make sale of the saide
     goodes, and that such debtes, duties and accountes, as can
     be lawfully required at my handes, shall be satisfied·[4]

1. The will is PRO, PROB 10/Box 163, Thomas
Caundish. The striking clarity of the writing,
almost wholly in Cavendish's secretary hand,
as established above, is even more marked
than in the manuscript account of the Last
Voyage.
2. On the *Roebuck*'s return see p. 39 above;
as is indicated there we do not know whether
she arrived alone or in company with the
Galleon Leicester.

3. The absence of punctuation after "Gorge" and
the space left was for the inclusion of the name of
Henry Seckford as a second executor if Gorges
wished this to be done.
4. This will states in general terms the responsi-
bilities of Gorges as executor; the manuscript
spells them out more specifically, which is why
it was taken into consideration in the proceedings
on the will and extracts from it accepted as a
codicil.

T. Thomas Caundish

In the name off God Amen. This is the last will and
Testament off me Thomas Caundish being at the making
hereoff in perfect mind and memory. first I bequeath
my soule into the handes off Almightie God, my maker,
Sauiour, and redemer, by whose death, passion, and
resurrection I hope to be saued, and to bee an inheritour
off his heauenly kingdome. Amen. Concerning my
goodes I dispose off them in maner and forme following. /
first (iff the Rocburke be returned into England) my will
is that the saide Rocburke and all such goodes off mine
as shall be found in her, or haue beene belonging to
her in whose handes soeuer they shall bee found
remaining, be deliuered to the handes off Tristram
Gorge Esquier to be disposed to such vses as this my
last will shall import. Also I further will that the
shipp called the Gallion Leicester, with all her goodes
whatsoeuer to her belonging be deliuered likewise
to the handes off the saide Tristram Gorge

Executor to dispose off these goodes according to this my
last will and testament. I also will that my
Executors, with speede conuenient, make sale off the saide
goodes, and that such debts, duties and accountes, as can
be lawfully required at my handes, shall be satisffied.

1   further my will is that, presently vpon the sale of theese
foresaide goodes, there be paide to William Goodrich one of
her maiesties Surgeons[1] the summe of one hundred markes
of good and lawfull money of England. And if my
5   saide Executor shall finde. (him self & all other duties
being satisfied) any ouerplus of the saide goodes to
remaine, I will that he deliuer the ouerplus of the
saide goodes remaininge to my sister Anne Caundish to be
vnto her as her owne proper goodes. / ~ And if it
10   happen that the two shippes, which are departed from me,
the one named the Desire, the other the Blacke Pinnes
do returne into England,[2] I dispose of them in forme
following· If they happen to bring with them any riches,
I will that my Executor seise vpon the saide shippes
15   and goodes, & that there be a true account taken of the
value of the saide goodes: out of which goodes I will
that euery aduenturer receiue proportionally to his
aduenture·[3] All which being satisfied, I dispose of such
goodes as shall remaine to me belonging[4] in maner
20   and forme following· / ~ first I will that the shippe
called the Desire with all her ordinance tacle and sailes
to her belonging, be deliuered by my saide Executor to
the handes of *Sir* George Carey knight to be
vnto him as his owne proper goodes·[5] / ~ Moreouer I
25   will that (if the saide Desire returning into England
bring any riches) the fourth part of such

1. We do not know what Thomas Cavendish's
relations with the surgeon were; he may simply
have been a friend, or he may have treated
Cavendish, and it is likely that he was a subscriber
to the voyage as well. Goodrich had been with the
earl of Leicester in the Netherlands in 1585
and was withdrawn by the Queen for her own
service. *Calendar of State Papers, Foreign, 1585–
1586* (London, 1921), p. 202. As "Master
Goodridge, her Majesty's Surgeon," he was employed in an investigation by the Privy Council in
1593. *Acts of the Privy Council, 1592–1593*
(London, 1901), pp. 181–82. As the Queen's
serjeant surgeon, he played a distinguished role
in the Barber-Surgeons' Company of London,
being master in 1594, and he continued to serve
James I as serjeant surgeon until at least 1610;
Sidney Young, *The Annals of the Barber-
Surgeons of London* (London, 1890), pp. 7, 18,
206, 329, 530–31, 537.

2. The *Desire,* of course, returned, but with no
other lading than she had had when she parted
from Cavendish. The *Black Pinnace* had been
lost when she parted company with Davis
(p. 36 above).

3. The third ship, which Cavendish, strangely,
does not mention was the *Daintie,* carrying a
cargo traded from and sacked from the Portuguese
at Santos. Though no formal record of her return
has been found, the reappearance of a man who
may have been in command of her (though the
evidence is not conclusive) may indicate she
arrived safely. See p. 106 above.

4. Written "belongimg."

5. The *Desire* went to Carey in the end, and was
privateering at sea for him, under Captain
William Irish, in 1596, K. R. Andrews,
Elizabethan Privateering (1964), p. 98.

further my will is that, presently vpon the sale off theese
foresaide goodes, ther be paide to William Goodrich one off
her maiesties Surgeons the summe off one hundred markes
off good and lawfull money off England. And iff my
saide Executor shall finde Him selff (, all other duties
being satisffied) any ouerplus off the saide goodes to
remaine, I will that he deliuer the ouerplus off the
saide goodes remaininge to my sister Anne Caundish to be
vnto her as her owne proper goodes. — And iff it
happen that the two shippes, which are departed from me,
the one named the Desire, the other the Blacke Pinnes
to returne into England, I disspose off them in forme
following. Iff they happen to bring with them any riches,
I will that my Executor seise vpon the saide shippes
and goodes, & that ther be a true account taken off the
value off the saide goodes: out off which goodes I will
that euery aduenturer receiue proportionally to his
aduenture: All which being satisffied, I disspose off such
goodes as shall remaine to me belonging in maner
and forme following. — first I will that the shippe
called the Desire with all her ordinance tarle and sailes
to her belonging, be deliuered by my saide Executor to
the handes off Sr George Cawy knight to be
vnto him as his owne proper goodes. — Moreouer I
will that (iff the saide Desire returning into England
bring any riches) the fourth part off such

1   goodes as shall belonge vnto me brought into England
    by the saide Desire, be likewise by my saide Executor
    deliuered to the saide *Sir* George Carey to be vnto him
    as his owne proper goodes· The remainder of all
5   goodes if any be brought by the saide shippes, belonging
    vnto me Thomas Caundish, I will that after
    my Executor hath satisfied him self and all
    aduenturers of such aduentures as they can lawfully
    claime, that the remainder of such goodes belonging
10 to me, be deliuered by my saide Executor to my
    Sister Anne Caundish to remaine to her as her
    owne proper goodes·[1]

Thomas Caundyssh

[seal][2]

15   Sined[3] and sealed in the presence of vs
                    Tho: Hammond
                    Steven Seaver
                    Robert Hues·[4]

1. It will be clear that under this arrangement Anne Dudley had no control whatever over the disposal of the estate, and that the chances of there being any substantial remainder for her when her brother's instructions had been carried out by Tristram Gorges were slight. It was for this reason that she fought so long to keep the administration of the estate in her own hands.

2. The impression of Cavendish's signet seal on the wax is sharp and fresh, but unfortunately it is not complete and consequently the crest and the upper part of the coat are lacking, even the lower quarterings not being wholly clear. Enough can be seen, however, to be certain that it bore his own arms. These were: Quarterly 1. Argent, three piles wavy Gules, the middle one reversed [Garnon]. 2. Sable, a chevron Or between three cups uncovered Argent [Cavendish]. 3. Barry of eight Argent and Gules, a lion rampant Or crowned per pale of the first and second [Brandon]. 4. Sable two bars Ermine between nine guttes d'eau [Potton]. Crest A wolf's head couped Azure collared and ringed Or. See *Visitations of Suffolk,* ed. Walter C. Metcalfe (Exeter, 1882), pp. 12–13.

3. A false start, "Sined Sealed and," has been crossed through.

4. While the signatures of Hammond and Hues are clear and strong, that of Stephen Seaver is quavering, and so reflects either his own poor physical condition or his unfamiliarity with the pen. Below, a note of the grant of probate on 14 February 1595[–6] is crossed through.

goodes as shall belonge vnto me brought into England
by the saide Desire, be likewise by my saide Executor
deliuered to the saide Sr George Carye to be vnto him
as his owne proper goodes. The remainder of all
goodes if any be brought by the saide shippes, belonging
vnto me Thomas Caundish, I will that after
my Executor hath satisfied him selfe and all
aduenturers of such aduentures as they can lawfully
claime, that the remainder of such goodes belonging
to me, be deliuered by my saide Executor to my
sister Anne Caundish to remaine to her as her
owne proper goodes.

Thomas Caundysh

Sined and sealed in the presence of vs

Tho: Hammond

Robert Hues.

Appendix I
The Sheviock-Antony Deed

The part of the parchment deed which now forms the inner side of the cover of the Cavendish manuscript is approximately 7.8 by 10.5 inches in size. Of this area a width of approximately half an inch is obscured by the sewing. The deed was trimmed at both ends and also at the top and the bottom to make it fit the paper gatherings, though it seems likely that the lower side is almost at the edge of the written area of the document. In transcribing what remains, the gap caused by the sewing has been filled conjecturally: in most cases the conjectures are almost certainly correct but a few remain guesses only. Similarly though a certain amount of reconstruction of the missing edges of the deed is possible, interpretation of the deed as a whole is difficult and may, owing to the need to make a number of assumptions, be faulty.

The document is a lease for lives, probably for three lives, of lands in the parishes of Sheviock and Antony, Cornwall, and apparently in the manor of Kerslake, by George Uppeton (or Upton), lord of the manor, to William Harrye, Agnes his wife, and Stephin (Stephen), whose surname is missing. It would appear that the lease involved a money rent of twenty shillings a year and a quit rent of two capons, with a heriot on the transfer of the land on the expiry of each of the lives for which the lease was granted. The grantor retained ownership of the timber on the land, which included elm trees, and preserved rights of access to it. Neither the identification of George Upton as the owner and lord of the manor of Kerslake nor the location of the manor in the parishes of Sheviock and Antony is certain, though certain probabilities emerge.

Thanks to Mr. P. L. Hull, county archivist of Cornwall, it has been possible to assemble a certain amount of collateral evidence about the places and persons named in the document. The manor of Antony was the hereditary property of Richard Carew of Antony, the historian and topographer: he had also acquired the manor of Sheviock and so at a time when the lease is likely to have been made owned the greater part of the parishes of both Sheviock and Antony. The precise location of the manor of Kerslake does not appear to be known, but a court roll of the manor of Kerslake exists in the Cornwall County Record Office, though it does not, unfortunately, contain the names of the lords of the manor in the later sixteenth century. The name Kerslake is mentioned in G. A. Kempthorne,

145

History of the Parish of Sheviock (Glasgow, [1934]), which also indicates that a family named Harrye were freeholders in the small
borough of Crafthole in the parish, though William, Agnes, and
Stephen are absent from the family names cited (pp. 21, 25, 38, 39,
69–70), and there is no mention of George Upton. There is a will,
dated 1603, in the County Record Office, of a man named William
Harris (who could be Harrye). There was a Cornish family of Upton
of Trelask in Lewannick, but there was no George in the branch
which married into the Lower family (Sir John MacLean, *History of
the Deanery of Trigg Minor,* 3 vols. [London, 1879], 3:384–86),
though there was a George Upton who leased property in Tredrea in
the parish of Parranaworthal (West Cornwall) in 1629 (document
in the Royal Institution of Cornwall, Truro). There were also Devon
Uptons, and a George Upton, whose inquisition post-mortem was
held in 1619–20 (PRO, IPM, 17 James I, Cornwall), but this does
not help with this particular lease. The inquiry, must therefore be
left inconclusive.

The point of making it is to see whether the document was one
which might well have been in Cavendish's hands when he set sail in
1591. This appears unlikely since his connections in the southwest
do not appear to have been considerable, even though deeds of little
value were used for other purposes than covering books, and the
presence of discarded parchment deeds among his stores is possible.
This in turn makes it improbable that the words on the other side of
the cover which can only partially be read, but which seem to be
"Thomas Cavendyshe his last voyage" are in one hand, while those
"written by him in 1592(?)" may be in another. We might conclude
that the cover was, most probably, added after the manuscript was
brought to England and while it was in Tristram Gorge's possession.
For this we have only the circumstantial evidence that Gorges lived not
too far from Sheviock and Antony at Budockshed, near Plymouth,
and had therefore local opportunity to obtain the deed after the
manuscript reached him. If we carry conjecture a little further we
might expect Gorges to have had the manuscript bound to protect it
during the long controversy which followed the appearance of the
Cavendish will and the need to place the manuscript which supported
the will before officials and the courts. Indeed the binding might
well have been done by Gorges's lawyers, who are somewhat more
likely to have had the deed in their possession than himself.

The transcription (numbers indicate beginnings of original lines)
which follows is necessarily defective: the conjectural additions at the
ends of the lines have even less authority than those made in the
medial break caused by the sewing, but some may prove useful if
further attempts to reconstruct the deed should prove worth while.

1. ... [of any]e and s[o manye] of theym all that [are amongst]
thapurten*au*nces nowe in the tenure or [occupacion] ... 2. ...
[par]ishes of Sheviocte and Antony and in bothe a[foresa]yd in the
saide Countie of Cornwall And all and [all manner] ... 3. ... remaininge or in anye wise appertaigninge or nowe p[artaigninge]
esteemed vsede occupied or enjoyed w*i*th the same ... 4. ... [the]
said George Vppeton his heires and assignes all the [oaks], Elmes
and Coppies or saleable woodes whatsoeuer nowe ... 5. ...
[grantinge] free and laufull libertie ingresse and [regress] and in all
meite and Convenient tymes, places and seasons ... 6. ... [as]
aforesaide and all other and singular the premisses [aforesaide] by
theise *pre*sent Indentures leasede and graunted w*i*th the ... 7. ...

[anye or euer]ye of theym for and duringe the tearme of the
[natural] liefes and duringe the liefe of the longeste liuer of euerye
or . . . 8. . . . of laufull moneye of Englande at and on the fower
me[ntioned and] accustomede tearmes and tyme of payment in the
yeare to w[hich] . . . 9. . . . [separate] and distincte portions to be
paide during th[e tym]es and estates aforesaide / And twoe Capons
yearelie at the . . . 10. . . . [to] his heires and assignes at and on the
deathe depa[r]cture gevinge vpe or other determynation of the
Interestes . . . 11. . . . [by waie] of a heriotte or sarleive / Prouidede
all [waies that] if the saide Agnes happen to dye or deceasse livinge
these . . . 12. . . . [Agnes] his wiefe or either of theym That then
by a[nye or everye] deathe of the saide Agnes and Stephin or either
of theym . . . 13. . . . hys heires and assignes to be yearelie holden
and k[epte . . .]nable waitinge within his Manour of Kerslake in the
parishe . . . 14. . . . mylles within the manour aforesaide And if
hit [the] saide yearlie rent of Twentie shillinges be vnpaide in
parte . . . 15. . . . [the] meaninge of theise presentes oughte to be
paide and [received] and beinge laufullie demaunded, and no
sufficient distresse . . . 16. . . . thereof (if anye happen to be) mayebe
levyede sa[tisfied and] paide That then and from thencefurthe hit
shall and . . . 17. . . . same and euery apparrell thereof resieue to and
have [vnto him] his former estate theise present Indentures and
seison [to] . . . 19. . . . And the saide William Harrye Agnes his
wiefe O[r the saide] Harrye and suruivour to theym or his or theire
assig[nes] . . . 20. . . . [pre]sented whatsoeuer to the graunted
premisses appert[aining] all neidefull or necessarie reparations at and
to hys or . . . 21. . . . [afo]resaide and so sufficientlie repayrede at
and in [place ther]eof shall have and give over the same / And the
saide . . . 22. . . . [that] the saide William Harrye Agnes his wiefe
[or to the said] Harrye and to and with euerye of theym by theise
presentes . . . 23. . . . by theise present Indentures leased and
graun[ted with all] theire appurtenaunces and euerye parcell thereof
[except before] . . . 24. . . . [euery]e of theire naturall liefes and
duringe the [liefe of the] longest liver of euerye or anye of theym in
maner and forme . . . 25. . . . nowe alreadye due and to be hereafter
due and goinge [out of the] premises as also againste all other people
and parsons for . . . 26. . . . premisses Conditions and reseruations
before in the [Indenture] expressede shall exonerate, acquite, and do
d[   ] . . . 27. . . . theise presentes And moreover know you that
the se[id] [George] Vppeton hathe in and by theise presentes
Constituted, . . . 28. . . . [in]steade to enter into and vpon the saide
Tenement [named in] the premisses or into somme parte thereof
in the name of t[he] . . . 29. . . . [there] of had and taken to deliver
peaceable possessi[on and sei]son thereof or somme parcell thereof
in the name of the w[hole] . . . 30. . . . accordinge to the purporte,
effecte tenour and true mea[ninge of] theise presentes / Ratefyenge,
acceptinge, Confirminge and all . . . 31. . . . [consente] of the
parties aforesaide to theise present I[ndentures] have Interchaunge-
ablye put theire signes and seales . . .

Appendix II
The Cavendish Will and Its Associated Documents

The original will of Thomas Cavendish in the records of the Prerogative Court of Canterbury, is now available in the Public Record Office, (PROB 10/163, Thomas Caundish, 14 February 1595–96). While the documents of the court were deposited in the Principal Probate Registry, Somerset House, the original wills were not available to inquirers; only the registers, where the Cavendish material was entered in Register Drake, Sentence 17 (now PRO, PROB 11/87), could be consulted. The original and the register entries can thus be studied together for the first time.

The will is contained in a gathering of two sheets of paper approximately 30.4 cm. by 40.5 cm. in size. These were folded in two and inserted inside one another so as to make a gathering of eight small folio pages 30.4 cm. by 10.2 cm. At some later period the gathering was folded horizontally in four so as to make a small packet 10.1 cm. by 20.2 cm., and it may have been in this form that it came to England, though it is probable it was contained, along with Cavendish's manuscript, in a joint package. As Cavendish left them, pages 1, 2, 6, 7 and 8 were blank, and the will was written on pages 3, 4, and 5, while on the blank pages a number of entries were made during and after the court proceedings in which the will and its associated documents were exhibited. The pages now contain:

P.1. Blank.

P.2. "Gorge &c *Contra* Dudley al*ias* Cavendish ext*racta* 2 sess*ione*," and below, reversed, "A reme*m*brance of certaine notes."

P.3. Above the will "Caundish R*eceptus*." The will, as on pp. 138–43 above, follows.

P.4. Will continued.

P.5. Will concluded, signed, sealed, and witnessed. Below is the entry "Probatum Su*m*mam xiiij° Feb*ruarii* 1595 iuxta &c coram *ma*gist*ro* Will*elmo* Lewin commissarii &c. Iura*men*te Galfridi Clerk not*ar*ii publice procura*tor*is Tristram Gorge exe*cutor*is &c de bonis &c Iura*men*te /."

P.6. This page bears the marks of the old horizontal folds, indicating that at one time it formed the outer page of the gathering. Across the second fold from the top is the old docketing entry "T Thome Candish ext*racta* 3da sess*ione* termin*o* pasche 1593 I." This would

148

seem to refer to the earlier proceedings on behalf of Anne Cavendish in 1593.

P.7. Extracts from the Thomas Cavendish manuscript, discussed pp. 41–43 above, which were accepted and entered as a codicil to the original will. They are headed "A remembraunce of certaine Notes conteyned in a wrightinge written with his owne hande sealed vpp by master Thomas Caundishe in a Certaine Packett with his will which togeather with his will was deliuered close and sealed vpp to Tristram Gorge Esquier./"

P.8. The "Notes" are concluded, ending: "Bearer herof 40li.Tho. Caundishe." This is followed by the formal entry, in Latin, of the grant of probate on 14 February 1595–96 of the will, with a codicil ("vnacum codicillo") to Walter Clerk, notary public, for Tristram Gorge, gentleman, setting aside the previous grant to Anne Dudley alias Caundish. All the matter in these pages, except for formal annotation, is carefully entered in the register.

The decree of the Prerogative Court of Canterbury, on parchment and in Latin, is sewn to the paper gathering. It declares that in the case of Tristram Gorge against Anne Dudley alias Caundish, sister, and also Beatrice Dennye, sister, intervening (the entries relating to her being inserted above the line), the probate of the will of Thomas Caundish is granted to Tristram Gorge and the decree is promulgated to this effect. It is signed by William Lewin, commissary of the court and attested by N. Stywarde. On the back, in a nineteenth-century hand, it is docketed "Will, Codicil and sentence Tho. Caundish February 1596."

Appendix III
Cavendish's Maps

Two charts, one of them in the Biblioteca Nazionale Centrale, Florence (Port.30), which will be referred to as the Florence map (pls. 7 and 8), and the other in the Algemeen Rijksarchief, The Hague (Leupe Inv.733), which will be referred to as The Hague map (pls. 9 and 10), throw light on Cavendish's achievement in his circumnavigation and on his objectives and his course in his last voyage. Both derive from lost Spanish originals. Those may have been captured by Cavendish during his first voyage or they could have been brought to England by some earlier explorer and taken over by Cavendish for his own purposes before he left England in 1586. Both the present maps contain insets of the southeastern tip of South America and the Strait of Magellan which could not have been drawn before the voyage. Both are most likely to have been constructed in their present form in or shortly after 1588. Both or either, in these or other copies, could have been taken on the Last Voyage and have been recovered when ships returned from it in 1593. In neither case, however, is there conclusive evidence that they left England in 1591 with Cavendish. The Florence map covers most of the South Atlantic, Brazil, and Spanish-claimed territory south of the Rio de la Plata, as well as the Strait, so that it applies to much of the second stage, the fatal one as it turned out to be, of the Last Voyage and was also traversed, under less unfavorable circumstances, on the circumnavigation. The Hague map repeats the depiction of the Strait, but is complementary to the Florence map in that it takes in the whole of western South America, Central America, and the Caribbean, and includes part of the California Peninsula (and had rather more before it was damaged at the top). It has the almost obliterated date "1588" near the top, under the "R" of "CANCRI," but no further legible inscription.

The maps themselves are very similar in construction and in the nature of their contents, while the fact that both have very similar insets makes it clear that they are directly complementary and were intended to be so from the time they were made. The style and manner of depicting detail are also closely parallel but there is no proof that they were drawn by the same man, though it is possible that they were. Mrs. Sarah Tyacke of the Map Library, British Library, has compared them for me with other examples of the Thames School of professional map and chart makers on which she is working and

150

considers that, in spite of their resemblances, both are drawn so very much within the conventions of the school that it would be possible for them to have been drawn by two different men. It is clear that the nomenclature on them was indeed the work of two men. The Florence map has the initials of the so-far unidentified "R. B." underneath the bar-scale, and if he wrote the inscription on the scale, which would seem almost certain, then his is most probably the hand of the map's nomenclature and it might reasonably follow that he drew the map as well. In the case of The Hague map the writing of the names is in Thomas Cavendish's own italic hand. Though Englishmen studied italic handwriting from a narrow range of text-books and their hands are consequently difficult to distinguish, there are enough similarities between the hand of the map and of the examples of his italic hand elsewhere to make it certain that he wrote the names himself, very neatly and professionally. He could also have drawn the map, but if he did so it was probably from a version by "R. B." or some other professional mapmaker rather than one derived directly by himself from the Spanish original, though of course other possibilities also exist.

The maps are very similar in size and could have formed part of the same collection. Both are on vellum and the Florence map is 75.5 cm by 95.5 cm, having its greater length from east to west; The Hague map is 74 cm by 58 cm, having its greater length from north to south. The intended scale of the Florence map, which extends from lat. 18°N to 55° S and from long. (approximately) 5°E to 70° W (though the northern coast of Brazil is cut off at about 47°), is 1:980,000 (10° lat. = 11.3 cm) (the real scale, it has been reckoned, varies very much from this except for parts of the shoreline), while the inset is 1:260,000 (10° lat. = 38.4 cm). The Hague map is on the intended scale of roughly 1:1,100,000 (10° lat. = 9.3 cm), though in practice varying greatly from it, and extends from lat. 30°N to 55° S and from long. 70°W (approximately) to (perhaps) 130°W, while the inset is approximately 1:300,000 (10° lat. = 37 cm). They are thus quite close to each other in scale. Both maps parallel very closely in nomenclature and latitudes the rutter of Thomas Fuller for the circumnavigation, as may be seen in Richard Hakluyt's *Principal navigations* 3 (1600):825–37. This indicates that they, or the Spanish originals from which they were compiled, were employed in the navigation of the parts they cover in 1586–87 or were correlated with the records obtained on this voyage. The data which the two maps furnish is very similar: the only major difference is that the Florence map has a bar scale and The Hague map has not.

Both maps also have a Dutch association. The Hague map does not ever seem to have been outside the Dutch archives (the number it carries in a hand later than the sixteenth century—No. 38—does not appear to be of value in placing it). The Florence map has a Dutch inscription on the back, "Brasilsche Caarte," and appears to have been brought from Holland with at least one other map in the Florence collection by the Grand Duke Cosimo III de Medici (1670–1723). The Dutch connection suggests quite strongly that both maps reached the Netherlands together and were separated only after a considerable period. One possible source for them is Richard Hakluyt. He was connected by marriage with Thomas Cavendish and obtained much material, very rapidly, on the circumnavigation; this could have included these maps, though there would necessarily be other copies left at Cavendish's own disposal. He was also in a good position to acquire materials on the Last Voyage: he was, for example, able

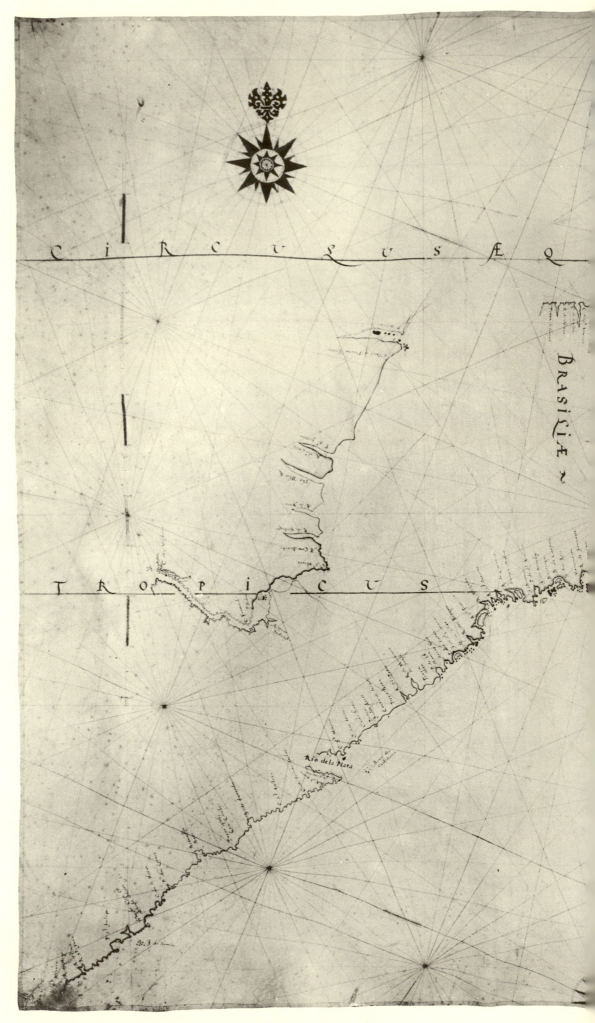

7. Cavendish's map of the South Atlantic, ca. 1588. Biblioteca Nazionale
   Centrale, Florence, Portolano 30.

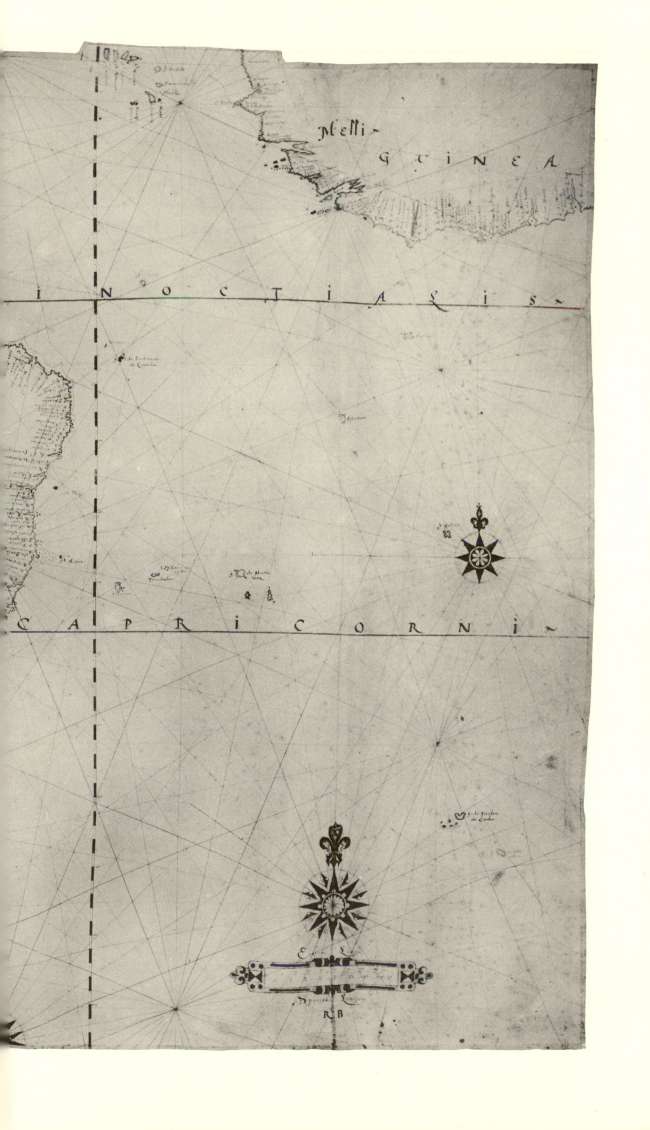

Melli-
GVINEA

i N O C T I A L i s

C A P R i C O R N i

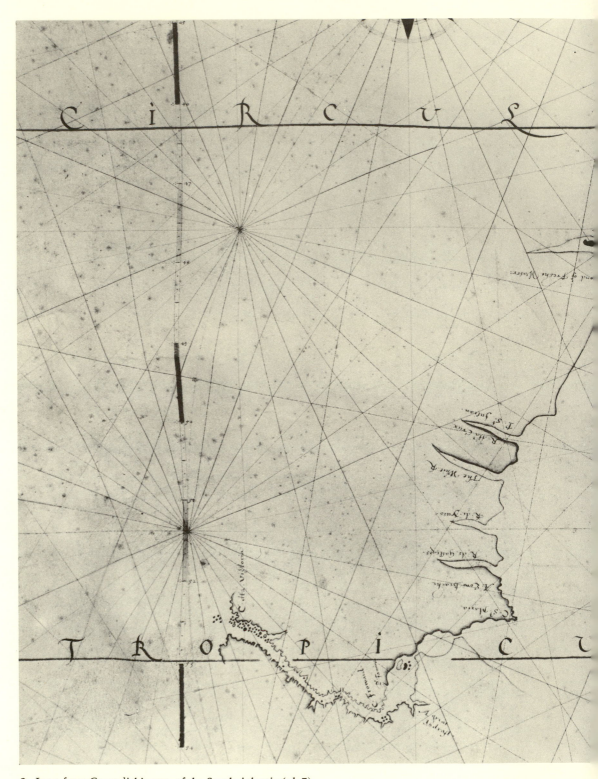

8. Inset from Cavendish's map of the South Atlantic (pl. 7)

to publish John Jane's pro-Davis narrative in 1600, and he may have already had (and withheld out of delicacy) the copy of the Cavendish manuscript which he passed on to Purchas, though of course he may equally well have acquired it after 1600. We know that in 1594–95 he was involved in collecting for the Dutch, through Emanuel van Meteren, materials on the Northeast Passage, and that he also passed on copies of the still unpublished narrative by Francis Pretty and the rutter of Thomas Fuller on the circumnavigation (as the letters in Algemeen Rijksarchief, Holland and West Friesland, Inv. 2687, Recueil Commercie, fols. 63–68, indicate); the consignment then sent could have included the two maps. Another possible source for the presence of the maps in Holland was their ownership by pilots who

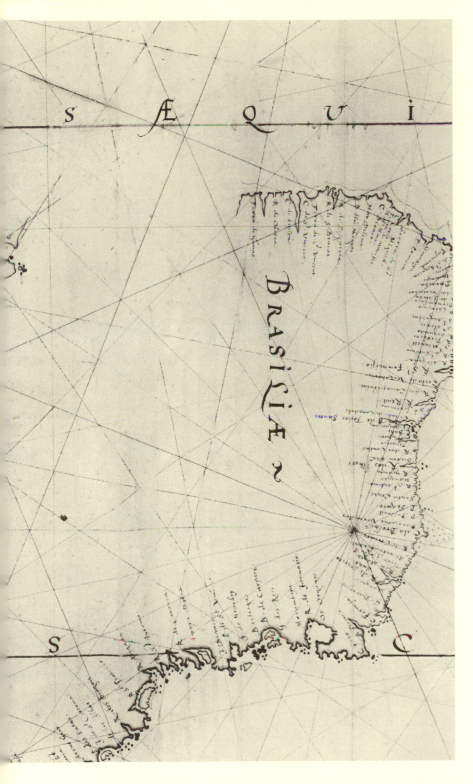

had served with Cavendish and who later helped to pilot the Mahu
and van Noort expeditions to the East Indies in 1598 for the Dutch,
such as the Captain Melis who died on van Noort's voyage (J. O. M.
Broek, *A Letter from Olivier van Noort* [Minneapolis: University of
Minnesota Press, 1957], p. 5; F. C. Wieder, *De reis van Mahu en de
Cordes,* 3 vols. [The Hague, Linschoten-Vereeniging, 1922–25];
J. W. Ijzerman, *De reis om de wereld door Olivier van Noort,* 2 vols.
[The Hague, Linschoten-Vereeniging, 1926]). One of these pilots, it
would seem, a Dutchman named Buteres who lived in Tower Street,
London, was said in 1606 to have sailed to the East Indies with Drake
and Cavendish and to have contracted to pilot the Portuguese fleet
to the East Indies in 1607 (PRO SP94/13, pt. 2, fols. 108–10).

The nomenclature southward from the Plate estuary on the

Florence map shows many signs of English adaptation and addition.
The majority of the names seem to have Spanish origins; most remain
untranslated but some are clearly turned into English, and English
names are given to some features not taken from the Spanish. The
forms are those of a not highly literate Englishman, e.g., Botombles
Baye and Whighe Cape, and are, we can assume, those of R. B. Those
inserted by Cavendish on The Hague map are certainly more literate
and those taken by him from the Spanish are more nearly accurate
in their forms. The Florence map has more names for the coastline
between Puerto de San Julian and Cabo de Santa Maria than The
Hague map, whereas the Florence map has less in the way of names
for the Strait itself. On The Hague map both the main map (where
the names are wholly Spanish ones) and the inset (where the
names are mixed Spanish and English) have a more abundant nomenclature. At the same time most of the English names on the Strait
are either to be found in the narratives of the circumnavigation or else
are descriptive; for example, "The First straight," "The seconde
straight," "A great Gulet." There is consequently little evidence that
any were added as a result of the experiences on the Last Voyage. But
it is at least probable that Cavendish had this map, or a version of it,
with him on the Last Voyage. John Davis, however, had the task
of making a more detailed chart of the Strait and this was probably
brought back by him to England in 1593, though it appears to have
been lost and no trace of its influence can be found on either of the
maps here considered, which clearly summarize the information

Nomenclature from Rio de la Plata to Cabo de la Victoria

FLORENCE MAP		THE HAGUE MAP	
Inset	Main Map	Inset	Main Map
	Rio de la Plata		
	C.S. Antonio		
	R. St. Anna		
	C. de Arenas Gordas		
	C. S^t. Andres		
	B. de Antegada		
	Point of the Low Lande.		
	Botombles Baye		
	Cabo de Matas		
	Whighe Oliues		
	Whighe Cape		
	I de Samson		
P Desier		Porte Desier	
A Pond of Freshe Water.			
		Seale y^a	
		P de Juan Serana.	
P.St. Julian.	P S^t. Julian	P S Julian.	
R dla Crux			
The Whit R		The White Riuer	
R de Ynes	R St Ynes		
	R of Crosse		
R de Gallegos.	R. Gallego		
A Low Beache		A lowe beach.	
C. S^t. Maria	C. St. Maria Bon	C Joye alijs C S Maria	C. St Maria
		The First straight	
		C Deseado	C. Deseada
		The seconde straight.	
		Y^{as} de Penguines	
A great Indraft		A great Gulet.	
P^o Famin		P Famin.	
C. Froward.		C. Frowarde.	C. Frowarde.
			C S Vincente
			R de S John
C dla Victoria.		C de la Victoria	C de la Victoria
		Caripana.	

9. Cavendish's map of the Pacific shore of America, ca. 1588, with nomenclature in his own hand. Algemeen Rijksarchief, The Hague, Leupe Inventory 733.

obtained on the first voyage, as has been indicated already, from Spanish charts modified by English experience.

Both maps have been published before and commented on expertly, but they have never been set out together and little comparison of them has been made. For the Florence map we depend on Guiseppi Caraci, *Tabulae Geographicae Vetustiores in Italia Adservatae,* 3 vols. (Florence, 1926–31), 1:10–12, pl. 34; for The Hague map, on F. C. Wieder, *Monumenta Cartographica,* 5 vols. (The Hague, 1925–33), 1:6–7, pl. 5. Dr. Helen Wallis, Librarian of the Map Library, British Library, Mrs. Sarah Tyacke, also of the Map Library, and Mr. J. Fox, Deputy Keeper of the Third Department, Algemeen Rijksarchief, have given much essential advice and help.

Index

Cavendish, Punta, Argentina, 56n
Cavendish, Richard (uncle), 9, 20
Cavendish, Thomas:Arms, 142n;
    character, 34–35, 46; early life, 7–8;
    family, 7; freeman, 20, 39; letters
    (see Carey, Henry; Walsingham,
    Sir Francis); death, 2, 5, 33, 34;
    (1585) voyage, 8–9; (1586–88)
    circumnavigation, 6, 7, 10–16, 60n,
    80n; bond, 3, 7; map, 38; (1591–
    92) voyage: assessment of, 38–39;
    commission, 19–20; financing of,
    44–45; objectives, 20–21;
    preparations, 18, 21
  manuscript, 33–34, 40, 46, 134n;
    authenticity, 1, 2–6; cover, 2, 3,
    145–46; handwriting, 2, 3, 4(pl.1),
    6, 33, 47; provenance, 1n;
    publication (see Purchas, Samuel,
    Pilgrimes); punctuation, 47–48;
    signatures, 3, 4, 5(pls. 1, 2), 132n;
    summary, "A Remembraunce," 6,
    41–43, 148, 149; watermark, 2
  will, 6, 33–34, 39–40, 128/129,
    136/137–140/141; codicil, 43,
    136n, 149; letters of administration,
    39, 149; probate, 41, 142n, 148–49;
    seal, 142n
Cavendish, William (father), 7; wife
    (see Wentworth, Mary)
Central America, 150
Chamberlain, Bryan, messenger, 41
Chambers, John, cook Galleon Leicester,
    31
Chancery, Inns of, London, 7
China, 16, 18, 62/63, 112n; map of, 14,
    20; trade prospects, 2, 7, 15, 20
Christopher, a Japanese, 14, 20, 21, 28
Ciudad Rey Felipe, 10, 68n; see also
    Port Famine
Clarke, John, 9; captain Galleon Dudley
    (1590), 19
Clerke, Walter, notary public, 41, 148,
    149
Clifford, George, earl of Cumberland, 7;
    voyages: (1586), 9–10; (1589), 18
Cocke, Abraham, captain Roebuck
    (1590), 19
Cocke, John (d.1574), 57n, 130n
Cocke, John, captain Roebuck, 57n;
    voyage (1591–92), 19, 22, 25, 52n,
    56/57, 114/115; illness, 30, 102/
    103, 126/127; death, 32, 33,
    128/129
Cocke, Richard, 34, 130/131
Cole, Elizabeth (wife of Tristram
    Gorges), 132n
Concepción, Chile, 12
Cornwall, 3, 145–47
Corpus Christi College, Cambridge, 7
Correa, Salvador de, 116n
Correia de Sá, Martim, 116n
Cosimo III, de Medici (d.1723), Grand
    Duke, 151
Cosmus, a Japanese, 14, 20, 21, 28
Cotton, Randolph, captain Daintie, 19,
    24, 27, 57n
Courtenay, Sir William, 40
crabs, 31
Crafthole, Cornwall, 146
Crosse, R. of (R dla Crux), 156
Cumberland, earl of. See Clifford, George
Curioso, Cabo, Argentina, 68n
customs duty, 16, 44

Dartmouth, Devon, 41
Davis, John, captain Desire, 19, 25; chart
    of Magellan Strait, 36–37, 38, 156;
    The seamans secrets, 20n, 23n, 41,
    54n
  voyages: (1585–87), 20; (1591–93),
    21n, 24, 16–27, 36–38, 41, 62n,

69n; accused of treachery by
    Cavendish, 26, 34, 41, 52/53, 54/55,
    68/69, 70/71
Dee, Dr John, 20
Denny (Denys), Beatrix, 43, 149
Denny (Denys), Thomas, 43
Deseado, Argentina, 10, 25, 56n, 60n,
    68n, 69n; see also Port Desire
Deseado, Cabo, Str. of Magellan, 10,
    11, 36
Desengaño, Punta, Argentina, 68n
"Doutrina christãa na lingua Brasilica,"
    22(pl.6), 23
Drake, Sir Francis, 40, 41; circumnaviga-
    tion (1576–80), 1, 6, 15, 20, 38;
    voyage (1595), 7
Dudley, Anne (alias Cavendish), 39, 40;
    lawsuit over will, 43, 142n, 148–49
Dudley, Robert (d.1588), earl of
    Leicester, 39, 140n
Dudley, Robert, 39, 43n
Dyke, Gwenyth, 3n, 7n, 18n

East Indies, 20, 45, 155; Cavendish in
    (1588), 15–16
East Suffolk Record Office, 3
Eaton, Thomas, customer of
    Southampton, 130n
Elizabeth I, of England, 17, 18, 39;
    court of, 7
Elliot, ——, of Ratcliffe, 34, 54n,
    130/131
Englefield, Sir Francis, 21n
Ersola, Thomas de. See Valladolid,
    Alonso de
Espírito Santo, Brazil, 29, 84/85,
    102/103; attacked by Cavendish
    (1592), 29, 86/87–100/101
Espíritu Santo, Cabo de, Philippines, 14

Falkland Is., S. Atlantic, 36
Fenton, Edward, voyage (1582), 10, 20
Fernandes, Simão, pilot, 8
Florence map, 10n, 150–51, 152(pl.7),
    154(pl.8), 158; nomenclature, 156;
    provenance, 151, 154–55; scale, 151
Flores Sea, Indonesia, 15
Foxcroft, Samuel: voyage to East Indies
    (1591), 20, 25
Frio, Cabo, Brazil, 21, 37
Froward, Cape, Str. of Magellan, 11, 24,
    156
Froward Reach, 11
Fuller, Thomas: rutter, 10n, 15n, 151,
    154

Gallego, River, 156
Gilbert, Adrian, 19, 20, 45
Gilbert, Sir Humphrey, 6
Gilolo. See Halmahera
Goa, India, 15, 80n
Godolphin, Sir Francis, 40
González de Mendoza, Juan, History . . .
    of China (1588), 17n
Good Hope, Cape of, 16, 20, 25, 45, 62n
Goodrich, William, surgeon, 33, 138/139
Gorges, Sir Arthur, M.P., 131n
Gorges, Edward, 9, 130/131, 131n
Gorges, Jane, 27n
Gorges, Tristram, 3, 21; executor of
    Cavendish's will, 33, 39–43,
    136/137, 148–49; instructions for,
    6, 34, 42–43, 128/129–132/133;
    wife, 42, 132/133 (see also
    Cole, Elizabeth)
Gradjagan, Java, 15n
Gravesend, Kent, 10
Gray's Inn, London, 7
Greenwich palace, 17
Grenville, Sir Richard, 6, 8, 19
Grimston Hall, Suffolk, 7
Guam, Marianas Is., 14

CHOICE   MAY '76

History, Geography &
Travel

CAVENDISH, Thomas. The last voyage of Thomas Cavendish, 1591–1592; the autograph manuscript of his own account of the voyage, written shortly before his death, from the collection of Paul Mellon, ed. by David Beers Quinn. Chicago, 1976 (c1975). 165p il map tab (Studies in the history of discoveries) 74-11619. 22.50. ISBN 0-226-09819-2. C.I.P.

It was Thomas Cavendish's misfortune that his most important sea voyage, the circumnavigation of the globe 1586–88, was overshadowed by the achievements of Drake and the defeat of the Spanish Armada. It was probably for those reasons that this young man set out in 1591 to accomplish something more spectacular by establishing trade between England and the Philippines, China, and Japan.   Instead, he never made it through the Strait of Magellan. Physically and emotionally exhausted, Cavendish vowed never to return to England. While aboard his flagship, he wrote an account of this ill-fated last voyage in which he tried to explain and rationalize why he failed. Cavendish was buried someplace at sea. First printed in an abbreviated version in 1625 by Purchas, the manuscript of this famous voyage mysteriously reappeared and is now reproduced. It was appropriate that the well-known Elizabethan scholar of overseas expansion, David Quinn, should

CAVENDISH

CHOICE   MAY '76

History, Geography &
Travel

be the editor. He has written a sound introduction that makes the entire voyage more meaningful. An important purchase for libraries with collections of voyages and travels.